MISSING

CHILDREN

MISSING

CHILDREN

BY MARGARET O. HYDE
AND LAWRENCE E. HYDE

FRANKLIN WATTS ■ 1985
NEW YORK ■ LONDON
TORONTO ■ SYDNEY

Photographs courtesy of
Adam Walsh Child Resource Center: pp. 4, 69;
Ken Siegel/Covenant House: p. 20;
UPI/Bettmann Newsphotos: pp. 23, 28,
44, 52, 60, 64; Child Find: p. 39;
FBI National Crime Information Center: p. 74.

Library of Congress Cataloging in Publication Data

Hyde, Margaret Oldroyd, 1917–
Missing children.

Bibliography: p.
Includes index.
Summary: Discusses missing children including those
who run away or are abducted by strangers or parents
and outlines ways to prevent and cope with this increasing
problem.
1. Runaway children—United States—Juvenile
literature. 2. Missing persons—United States—Juvenile
literatue. 3. Child abuse—United States—Prevention—
Juvenile literature. 4. Child molesting—United States—
Prevention—Juvenile literature. 5. Abduction—United
States—Prevention—Juvenile literature. 6. Kidnapping,
Parental—United States—Prevention—Juvenile literature.
[1. Runaways. 2. Missing children] I. Hyde, Lawrence E.
II. Title.
HV741.H89   1985   362.7'4   85-7323
ISBN 0-531-10073-1

5012583

CONTENTS

MISSING

CHILDREN

To Molly Reeder Hyde

CHAPTER 1

A NATIONAL EPIDEMIC

The problem of missing children has long been a serious social concern in the United States. The Department of Health and Human Services estimates that between 1.3 million and 1.8 million children and young people disappear from their homes each year. Most of these children and teenagers are runaways, but estimates of the number who are abducted by strangers range from 25,000 to 500,000. Of those who disappear, many fall victim to homicide.

Experts predict that one in four girls and one in ten boys will be molested or raped by the time they reach adulthood. Recent studies have shown that large numbers of children who have been criminally or sexually exploited were missing from their homes when the act of exploitation occurred.

When a child or young adult is discovered missing, it can mean several things. The reason for the disappearance used to make a great deal of difference in the timing and the extent of a search. Missing might mean stranger abduction, and if a child was young, police cooperation was good. Missing might mean a runaway. Police showed little interest in such cases, even when parents showed great concern. Parental abduction of a child was another category that received scant attention from police. When a child was stolen by one parent from the legal custody of another, authorities were prone to think of this problem as a family affair that was not their concern. Although there has been a great sensitivity to the problem of missing children more recently, to some degree all of the former attitudes still prevail.

Statistics about missing children vary greatly because they are based on different age groups, and different localities. In most statistics, young adults are classified as children, but this is not always the case. In addition to the difficulty in deciding at what age a boy or girl is no longer to be known as a child, there is the problem of underreporting of missing persons. A child reported missing in one state may not be on the list of missing children in another state. But no matter how one counts, there are far too many missing children and teenagers, and there is a great need for a better system of reporting those who disappear.

WHO ARE THE MISSING?

■ *Runaway Youth*

Within the next hour, more than 200 boys, girls, and teenagers of all ages may be reported missing in the United States. Usually, their parents are assured by the police that their children have just run away and that they will be back when they are hungry and frightened. Certainly it is true that many children who are reported missing are runaways, and most of them are found. However, the number that run away and are never found is alarming.

Many young people who disappear are "pushouts" or "throwaways" who are turned out by parents who do not want them or who run away because their home situation is intolerable. It is estimated that 60–70 percent of today's runaways come from homes in which they have been abused.

■ *Victims of Parental Abductions*

One of the most common reasons for the disappearance of children is kidnapping by a parent who is dissatisfied with a custody arrangement or by a parent who seeks revenge against an ex-spouse. In a recent study that was conducted by Professor Richard Gelles of the University of Rhode Island, the number of incidents of parental kidnapping was estimated to be much greater than previously believed. This study estimated that between 313,000 and 626,000 children are abducted by parents each year. Many of these children suffer great emotional strain, being forced to live under an assumed name, and moving frequently from place to place to avoid detection by the parent from whom they were snatched.

■ *Victims of Stranger Abductions*
Many thousands of other youths are missing because they have been abducted by strangers. The children and teenagers who survive a period of abduction or separation from their families are left with lasting emotional and physical problems. For some of them, the suffering ends in death. Abductions by strangers are less common than parental kidnappings, but the reported sexual abuse and murder, in many cases, are hard to believe.

Consider the plight of the thousands of children who disappear without a trace each year in the United States alone. No one knows if they are living or dead. Parents and other relatives live from day to day, many searching frantically as they imagine the horrible things that could be happening to their child. When they learn the fate of other missing children, their hopes are not raised. If there are no clues left behind, there is only a very low probability that they will succeed in their search unless there is some action taken by the missing person. The parents, friends, and other concerned people ask themselves the same questions again and again. Are the children being tortured, forced to live in situations in which they are being sexually abused, or have they just lost their memories and cannot find their way home?

Many of the parents who search for their children ask themselves why anyone could be so cruel as to abduct a child. Children are abducted for a variety of reasons that

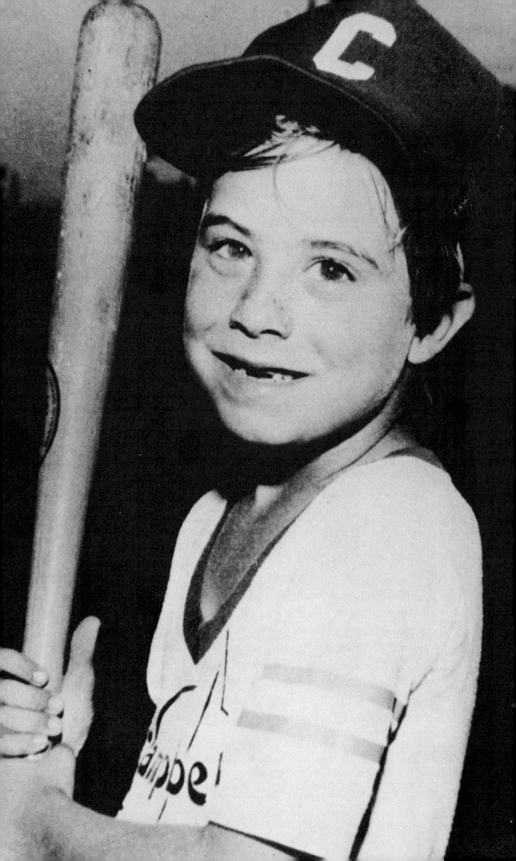

include an emotional need for a child, black market adoption, parental kidnapping from an ex-spouse, and for sexual abuse. A small percentage of the children who are missing are kidnapped by people wanting to replace a lost child. But to the parents whose child has been taken, the reason is unimportant.

Law enforcement agencies estimate that as many as 5,000 people a year, half of them children, are murdered without apparent motive; these children are murdered by pimps who live by exploiting children, by pedophiles (people who are sexually attracted to children), and by other deviants. In many cases, one person, a serial murderer, accounts for a large number of crimes. Reports indicate that thirty men were responsible for murders of from six to sixty people each during the last ten years. Lack of an efficient central information system has been blamed for helping these killers to prey on victims in a number of different states in the country.

■ *Lost Children*
Some children join the ranks of the missing because they become lost or victims of accidents and cannot find help. Children who are lost account for a far smaller number of the missing, and fortunately many of them are found by fast community action. For example, six-year-old Shannon Evans disappeared from a camp in Vermont where he, his father, and brothers were staying. He was last seen about 3 p.m. when he left his family to head back to camp from a nearby area.

Adam Walsh, abducted in 1981
from a Florida department store,
was memorialized in a television
movie that brought the problem
of missing children to the attention
of millions of viewers.

By eight o'clock that night, a search party of about seventy people was organized. Before sixteen hours had passed, 200 people were part of the search party that included local volunteers, state police, game wardens, Border Patrol, Red Cross workers, local ambulance workers, fire departments from three towns, and the Army National Guard with their helicopters. A farmer found the frightened boy walking along a highway the morning after he disappeared. He had wandered into the deep woods near the campsite and could not find his way back.

This story demonstrates the type of cooperation engendered by a crisis situation involving a child. This is especially true in small communities that are considered safe neighborhoods. When a local child is taken, large numbers of people may become involved in the search. When a fourteen-year-old newsboy was abducted while on his paper route, sexually assaulted, stabbed, and murdered, there were 700 leads and 1,500 interviews that led to the arrest of his seventeen-year-old assailant. As a result of his murder, an urgent call for action arose that would speed the search of missing children.

EFFORTS TO FIND MISSING CHILDREN

■ *Lack of Cooperation*
by Legal Agencies
Through the years, many voices have been raised in angry protest about the lack of cooperation in efforts to find missing children. Parents rarely found strong efforts being made by legal authorities until valuable time had passed, and they were certain that the missing person was not a runaway. Since prompt action is an extremely important factor in locating a missing child, this delay increased the number who were never found.

Running away and abduction has long been considered a local problem, even though many children were abducted across state lines. The Federal Bureau of Investigation has often been accused of not wanting to clog its computers with runaways and other missing children. Until recently, it was easier to trace a stolen automobile than a kidnapped child.

- *New Awareness of the Problem*
New awareness of the problem of missing children and teenagers has recently led to the use of better methods of searching for a person who has disappeared. How pressure was brought to bear on legal authorities, from the local to the federal level, is the story of the work of many people. Important first steps have been made, but the problem of missing children and young people remains a serious social problem.

- *Missing Children Act*
A milestone in the work of advocates for the missing was the passage of the Missing Children Act of 1982. It enables a parent, legal guardian, or next of kin of a missing juvenile to inquire directly of the Federal Bureau of Investigation as to whether or not a record of the missing person has been entered in their computer network, the National Crime Information Center (NCIC) missing persons file. If no entry has been made, pressure may be brought to bear on local authorities to make the entry, and if they refuse, the FBI will enter the record of the missing person. (See Exhibit 1.)

In testimony before Congress in support of the passage of this Act, it was pointed out that only 10 percent of those reported missing were entered into the Federal Bureau of Investigation's information system. A major reason for this omission included reluctance on the part of local police departments to enter missing children on the NCIC missing persons file because of the attitude that missing children were a "domestic dispute." A lack of awareness by local authorities about the availability of this system, and the unwillingness of the FBI to increase their manpower in the periodic updating of their NCIC files accounted for the lack of records.

MISSING PERSONS REPORT
AND
REQUEST FOR NATIONAL CRIME INFORMATION CENTER ENTRY

Name_____

Address_____

D.O.B._____Age_____Race_____Sex_____Comp_____

Height_____Weight_____Physical Build_____

Eye Color_____Hair Color_____Hair Style_____

Facial Hair and Style, (Beard, Mustache, etc.)_____

_____

Scars_____

Birth Marks_____

Tattoos_____

Condition of Teeth_____

Eye Glasses_____Style_____Contact Lenses_____

Fingerprint Class_____

Other_____

Clothing Last Seen Worn_____

_____

Jewelry Worn_____

Date Last Seen_____Where Last Seen_____

Possible Destination_____

Possibly Traveling With_____

Reporting Agency_____Telephone_____

Case Number_____Date Entered N.C.I.C._____

Car Information_____

_____

EXHIBIT ONE

The passage of the Missing Children Act called for the establishment of a national clearinghouse for missing children and unidentified deceased individuals. However, this is only effective if it is widely used. The Act does not direct the federal government to actively search for a missing child or teenager. This still remains a local responsibility.

■ *Need for Solutions*
The passage of the Missing Children Act was only the first step in moving toward solutions of a problem that has become epidemic in proportion. Continued action by many individuals is helping to improve communication among various agencies of the criminal justice system, juvenile justice system, and social agencies. If gaps in these systems were tightened, many child exploiters who move from one community to another would not profit from the lack of information sharing among law enforcement systems. Although it is difficult to grasp the scope of the missing children problem, it is not difficult to join the forces that are beginning to make some progress in attacking this national epidemic.

CHAPTER 2

A GROWING PROBLEM —OUR NATION'S RUNAWAYS

"I'll show them they can't treat me like that. I'll run away." This is a common threat made by young people who feel that their parents are too strict, make them work too hard, refuse to buy the things they feel that they need, and/or abuse them. The act of running away may be precipitated by a small event, but it is usually the result of long-term family problems. Physical, emotional, and sexual abuse play a part in a very large number of the lives of those who leave home. Although a small percentage of runaways are searching for glitter and glamor in the city in an effort to escape the boredom of a quiet neighborhood, the majority of runaways are "throwaways" or "pushouts." In such cases, their families may be glad the child has disappeared.

Although no one knows exactly what percentage of runaways become missing children, it is known that many runaways are not reported as missing children because they leave a home in which they are not wanted. When a child or teenager is reported missing, one of the first questions asked by police is whether or not the boy or girl might have run away.

No matter what the plan, there is usually a combination of reasons why a child or teenager takes flight. The search for adventure or the escape from home conditions that are unbearable are often the explanations given by an individual runaway. Most young people only plan to stay away a day or two and travel less than ten miles from home, but others hope to find a new lifestyle in a distant place and never return to the home they have learned to hate.

RUNAWAYS JOIN THE PERMANENTLY MISSING

Tens of thousands of the estimated two million or more young people who run away from home each year disappear permanently. It is no wonder that those concerned with the problem of missing children are involved in efforts to prevent their running away.

The missing children register of a local awareness program describes 268 cases from forty-three states. Of these, 103 cases were considered to be parental kidnappings, 65 children were classed as runaways, and 100 did not fall into either of the above categories. Twenty-seven of the runaways had been found alive, and thirty-eight were still missing.

CHANGING ATTITUDES TOWARD RUNAWAYS

■ *Colonial Times*
Attitudes about runaways have changed through the years. In colonial times, a runaway was regarded as a loss to the family's work force as well as an offender against family and God. Charles Loring Brace, in 1880, considered runaways to be the class of a large city that was "most dangerous to its property, its morals, and its political life." Some of these children were probably abandoned or pushed out of their homes, but others may have been sorely missed by their families. Many captured runaways of that time were confined in almshouses with the poor, the mentally disturbed, and the chronically ill. Brace and his fellow reformers believed that

they were performing a great charity by shipping large numbers of runaways to "the best of all asylums, the farms of western settlers." No one knows how many children found a better life with a new family who accepted them as their own, but it seems likely that many labored hard and long for their keep.

■ *The Nineteenth Century*
The belief that runaways needed to be reformed in a prison-like institution called "a school of reform" or "house of refuge" persisted for many years. Toward the late 19th century, attitudes toward children changed. Laws were passed prohibiting child labor and enforcing school attendance. The newly established juvenile justice system supposedly adopted the role of a caring parent by taking the children who had run away from their homes under its wing, where they could be helped. However, the runaway still was considered delinquent and often was described as a surly, assaultive, destructive, and antagonistic child. It was admitted, however, that some of these children were oversubmissive and docile.

■ *The Twentieth Century:*
A Punishable Crime
By 1968, running away was considered a punishable crime for anyone under the age of 18 and young people who were reported missing by their families were returned if they were located. Generally, child abuse at home was not considered a factor that may have precipitated the child's flight from the family and was often ignored.

THE 1960s: LACK OF COOPERATION BY PUBLIC AUTHORITIES

When a parent reported a missing child in the 1960s, the police reaction was often uncooperative. Consider the following case in which only the names have been changed.

When Michael Jones did not come home from school one day, his mother was concerned. When she had not heard from him by midnight, she became so alarmed that she called the police to report him missing. She was very upset when the police told her that they could not do anything to help until Michael had been missing for 24 hours.

When her son did not return the next day, Mrs. Jones called again. By now, she was in a state of panic. Something terrible must have happened to Michael. Even though she and her son had many disputes, Mrs. Jones assured the police that Michael would never run away. When the police detective asked for permission to inspect Michael's room for clues to his possible whereabouts, Mrs. Jones was glad that someone finally appeared to be making an effort to find her missing son.

Examination of Michael's room uncovered evidence of drug use. The police detective's reaction to this was casual. He told Mrs. Jones that large numbers of teenagers were leaving home for the city where they joined groups of protesters. The police did not have time to try to track down every child who ran off to the city to live with other flower children. But, he added, she was not to worry. Her son would run out of money, get tired of the hippie scene, and return home. The police bulletin boards, he explained, were so cluttered with pictures of missing children who had run away that no more pictures could be added. There just was not much that the police could do to help parents find their missing teenagers.

For many of the young people who were reported missing in the decade of the '60s, life centered around a protest of material things and politics, and promoted sex, drugs, music, and casual living. The "flower children," as they were sometimes called, preached peace and love, caring for each other as best they could on limited amounts of money. Many helping professions formed networks of human services that provided soup and bread along with free medical care for these young people. When the excitement of experimenting with new lifestyles wore off, many of the missing sons and daughters returned to their former homes to continue their personal struggles.

FAMILIES IN CRISIS
IN THE 1970s AND 1980s

By the 1970s the majority of children who were missing from their homes by their own choice left home for different reasons. The runaways of the '70s and the '80s are viewed largely as children and young people who come from families in crisis. Such was the case of Jane and her friend, Sara.

■ *Jane and Sara: A Case Study*
Jane and Sara discussed running away from home many weeks before they actually carried out their plans. The episode that made them take action was a beating from Jane's stepfather when she returned home one night, an hour after curfew. He threatened to lock her in the house each night after six o'clock for the next month, to punish her for what he called her sex life with scum. Jane knew that her stepfather was jealous of the boys she dated and that he wanted her all for himself.

Jane had tried to stop her stepfather's sexual advances for several years. Her mother would not believe Jane when she went to her for help, and that made Jane feel even worse. She hated this man who took her own father's place but treated her as if he owned her body and could use it whenever he wished. Jane never told anyone other than her mother about her problem until one night when Sara spent the night at her house and her stepfather tried to fondle both of the girls. Sara was a good friend; she understood.

Sara had her own problems at home. She hated her mother, who was separated from Sara's father and who refused to let Sara visit him. Her mother brought home a series of men to live in the house they had shared with Sara's father and she expected Sara to treat them nicely.

—15

For both Jane and Sara, running away from home seemed to be the only solution. After Jane's beating, the girls arranged to steal all the money they could find in their homes, board the bus, and head for New York where they hoped to pass for teenagers who were old enough to work. They would stay at the YWCA when they arrived and look for jobs in the local restaurants.

The first problem arose when the desk clerk at the YWCA told them they were under age and could not stay there without an adult. They decided to find a place to eat, and they would then discuss their next move over dinner. Perhaps someone in the restaurant could suggest a safe and inexpensive place for them to stay.

After walking for a long time, Jane and Sara found a restaurant that was not crowded and did not look very expensive. They ordered hamburgers and asked the waitress if she knew of a hotel where they could spend the night. She was very understanding and told the girls that she had come to New York the year before and had had a similar problem. She couldn't help them but she had a friend who might. The waitress suggested that they come back when she was finished with her shift and she would introduce them to her friend.

Jane and Sara felt much better, so they went to a movie and then looked in the store windows until it was time for the waitress to finish work. When they returned to the restaurant, they were introduced to Sam, a boy about their own age. He confided that he had been a runaway himself. Now he had a great job and a place of his own. They could go to his place, cook some hamburgers, and listen to some records with him if they liked. They could even sleep in his spare room for a few days until they found jobs. Jane and Sara jumped at the invitation. They were so afraid that a fatherly-type man would pretend to help them and that they would find themselves involved with him sexually. They were smart enough to avoid people who offered runaways a place to stay and smooth-talked them into juvenile prostitution. Sam was a kid himself, so they felt safe with him.

At Sam's place, the atmosphere was relaxed. The girls began looking for work, but Sam told them this was not necessary. He had arranged for them to work for a friend of his. When they discovered that they were expected to provide sexual favors for him and for others who came to the apartment, the girls tried to leave. They soon found that they owed a large bill and would be physically restrained if they tried to go. Even when they offered to pay for the large bill that Sam said they owed him for room and board, they were threatened with bodily harm. They discovered, too late, that Sam was a runner who recruited girls for an older man, a pimp, who represented himself as a protector of young girls. This man arranged for customers who supposedly would never hurt the girls during their sexual encounters and he would arrange bail for his girls when they were arrested for prostitution. Sara and Jane discovered that they had become captives in a system of juvenile prostitution.

RUNAWAYS IN URBAN CENTERS

The fate of Sara and Jane was similar to that of thousands of girls who run away to large cities and, in some cases, to smaller towns. Many of these girls are approached in less than five minutes after they have stepped off the bus. Although some of the runaways escape the "helpful friends" who offer assistance in finding jobs and who provide them with a temporary place to stay, only a small percentage make it on their own or receive help from a shelter.

Some runaways experiment with living in abandoned buildings where they have no electricity or running water. They brush their teeth in public restrooms and eat their meals at Skid Row missions. Boys and girls have been seen diving for food in trash bins behind restaurants. Many turn to drug dealing, stealing, and peddling sex in order to survive.

Boys who sell their bodies are more likely to work independently than girls. Large numbers of young boys make themselves available to older men who involve them in a variety of sexual acts. While some of these boys are afraid to go home again because of what they have become, others know they are not wanted at home.

Boy prostitutes have short careers. Once their childhood has gone, they are no longer as desirable to the people who are involved in the multi-million-dollar business of exploiting children. They may become runners like Sam, or they may join those who exploit their children. In any case, they appear to have an undesirable future if they live to adulthood.

Police believe about 20,000 runaways are on the streets of New York at any one time. Although it is difficult to obtain reliable statistics, as many as 1.2 million children are believed to be involved in pornography and prostitution in the United States each year. Some are so young that they receive their rewards in the form of candy or toys.

Many child prostitutes are introduced to their lifestyle through child pornography. They may be invited to model in the nude and given a reward. Then they graduate to movies involving sexual acts with other children or with adults. "Kiddie porn" is a means of support for some of the runaways, but there are some children who enter this world through the arrangements made by their parents or by abduction.

EMOTIONAL EFFECTS ON SEXUALLY EXPLOITED CHILDREN

A report by the United States General Accounting Office titled "Sexual Exploitation of Children: Problem of Unknown Magnitude" explores the problem of child prostitution and pornography and the effects they have on children. One of the conclusions of this study is that the children who are robbed of their normal childhood through sexual exploitation grow up suffering severe emotional problems that cannot be understood by people who have not experienced their tragic situation. Without therapy, they may suffer throughout their entire lives. And some, of course, join the ranks of the missing because they do not live to grow up.

CHAPTER 3

FINDING
RUNAWAYS

The National Network of Runaway and Youth Services says they tie the shoes of some of the world's fastest runners. Many of the people who work with runaways wish they could somehow catch them in a net to protect them. The best way to protect them would be preventing them from running away in the first place. The runners should be running toward something rather than just away from their troubles. If life at home is so bad that they must leave, let them leave for a better place rather than the stark life of the street. Those who work with runaways tell story after story of children and teens who have been shot full of drugs, tortured, imprisoned, and killed.

TIME FACTOR IN
LOCATING RUNAWAYS

Whether or not young people have any awareness of the risks, they continue to run away. The majority return home within a few days. Some may return home or go to other homes with the help of the police and/or social agencies within a few weeks, and some are never heard from again.

The time factor seems to be the dividing line between those who return home or find help for their problems and those who become permanently missing and victims of sexual exploiters or other deviants.

HOMELESS YOUTH

Although only a minor percentage of runaways are never heard from again, the number of individuals who disappear is large enough so that running away is considered to be a major social problem. Father Bruce Ritter, founder and president of a shelter for runaways and homeless youth called Covenant House, recently told conference delegates from twenty-eight countries that "informed guesstimates" place the number of homeless youth throughout the world in the tens of millions. According to the director of the United States Runaway and Homeless Youth Program, recent estimates of the number of homeless and runaway youth in the United States alone range between 733,000 and 1,300,000. Most of them face poverty, hunger, shattered family lives, rootlessness, and exploitation.

HOTLINES TO PROTECT RUNAWAYS

Hotlines for runaways help to protect children from the dangerous world of the missing and also help to reunite them with their parents or provide an alternate place to live. Two national runaway hotlines began in the '70s. One grew out of the public outrage that followed the discovery of a sex ring involving about 300 young men and boys, many of whom were runaways.

*Father Bruce Ritter, counseling
a runaway teenager at Covenant
House in New York City*

—21

RESPONSE TO MASS MURDER

In the summer of 1973, the bodies of a number of children who had been reported missing in Houston, Texas, were discovered buried in a rented boat shed. Further investigation and a wider search uncovered a total of twenty-seven murdered victims. Evidence showed that the leader of the sex ring responsible for these murders was often called "The Man with the Candy" for he made friends with children at a candy store.

In that summer of 1973, some Houston parents had reported that their children were missing and they accused the police of neglecting to search for them. But at that time, about 5,000 youth were reported missing in Texas each year, and many of the murder victims lived in a neighborhood where 150 to 200 juveniles were reported missing annually. The police contended that they were understaffed and swamped with missing children reports.

Parents, police, and the large numbers of people who read about the murders felt strongly that some kind of action had to be taken to intervene in the lives of runaways by providing some kind of service that would help to protect them. As a direct response to these mass murders, Texas Governor Dolph Briscoe introduced the national runaway hotline that was originally called Operation Peace of Mind. Now known as the Runaway Hotline, it continues to help runaways and the families of missing children.

CHANNELS OF COMMUNICATION

Another effective hotline is the National Runaway Switchboard, which evolved from a local telephone crisis center and now is supported by the federal government as part of the Runaway and Homeless Youth Act. It makes use of television public service announcements, articles in national newspapers and magazines, along with posters in bus terminals, libraries, and other places where young people may notice

A counselor taking a call for the hotline at the National Center for Missing and Exploited Children

them. It is listed on page 85 at the end of this book, or can be obtained by calling the operator.

Both the Runaway Hotline and the National Runaway Switchboard answer calls twenty-four hours a day, seven days a week and are providing a neutral channel of communication between runaway youth and their parents or guardians. In addition to message services, the Switchboard supplies referral services to one of several hundred shelters throughout the United States that provide temporary bed, board, and counseling. As with other hotlines, the volunteers and trained operators who answer the phones are concerned with getting the runaway off the street and into a safe shelter as quickly as possible.

In addition to the hotlines mentioned, Child Find provides a toll-free national hotline for missing children. This organization tries to help parents who are searching for children and children who are searching for their parents. Although many of these youths who are trying to go home are the victims of parental abduction, some of them are runaways who have lost track of their parents.

There are also many local hotlines whose numbers are posted in areas frequented by young people. You may have noticed such numbers in video arcades, heard them on public service announcements on radio or television, or seen numbers listed in telephone directories.

AID TO YOUTH IN TROUBLE

Many children who disappear do not realize the difficult problems they may encounter. Mark is a fifteen year old who had run away from his home in Pennsylvania two days before calling the hotline. He had been having trouble both at school and with his father, so he took the bus to New York hoping to live with a friend. Since he could not find the friend, he called the hotline saying he wanted to "get off the streets" and would like to speak to a counselor. He spent several days at Under 21, the famous shelter begun by Father Bruce Ritter, after which he was able to return home and receive counseling in his own home town. No one knows what might have happened to Mark if he had not been "found" through the hotline.

Counselors at hotlines provide emotional support, help callers explore options, and help them to improve their own problem-solving skills. For those who seek reconciliation and want to return home, arrangements are made that often involve the help of other agencies. Efforts are made to change the situations that caused the person to run away in the first place. For some children, arrangements must be made for care outside the home, possibly with a foster family or relative.

HOTLINES MAINTAIN CONFIDENTIALITY

Every hotline call is unique, but many conversations dealing with the problem of family abuse or neglect, poor communication, alcoholism and drug abuse, unemployment, and lack of education are common. All hotlines maintain confidentiality, although there is some variation in what this word means locally. Consider the following case.

Suppose a young girl has run away from home. She does not want to return home as yet, but she wants her parents to know that she is safe. She calls the hotline toll free. The phone rings and a volunteer answers, giving his or her name. Without having her family know where she is, the girl can leave a message that she is safe, or any other message. She tells the volunteer the name, the address, and the phone number of the person she wants her message to reach. Only the exact message is relayed, although the volunteer will ask the girl's name and some identification that is best known to both her and her family. The volunteer suggests that she call back later to see if there is a message for her. All the information remains confidential.

HELPING PARENTS OF RUNAWAYS

Although hotline personnel do not search for children or force them to return home even when they know the whereabouts of a child or young adult, some of them do help parents of runaways in their search. Ms. Johnson, the parent of a runaway, called the hotline to report that her fourteen-year-old daughter had run away two days before. The girl and her friend took her father's car, leaving a note that she needed some time to think. Ms. Johnson explained that there had been fighting at home between herself and Sally's father, but now she was more nervous and anxious than ever. What should she do?

The Hotline counselor provided some direction for Ms. Johnson. They advised her to think clearly, call the police, search for clues, publicize Sally's disappearance, and if Sally called, show love and concern rather than fear and anger. They told her to call the National Runaway Switchboard to leave a message in case Sally called. The counselors at hotlines are supportive to both young people and parents, for they are eager to locate the runaway and to minimize the dangers involved when he or she is on the streets.

FAMILY REUNION MONTH

Many organizations who are working to combat the problem of runaway youth have joined together to promote Family Reunion Month. This month-long campaign lasts from Mothers Day in May to Fathers Day in June, during which time every runaway who has not had contact with his or her family during the previous year is urged to contact them in some way. The contact might be by phone, letter, card, or by a mail-o-gram sent to one of the groups that sponsor the program, thus keeping the whereabouts of the person undisclosed. They pledge to maintain the privacy of the sender and will forward his or her message. They volunteer to forward letters to the missing children, teens, or young adults as well. Although these agencies will not ask questions, or make any accusations, they hope to be especially helpful to young people who are wondering what kind of reception they would find if they returned home after a prolonged absence.

During one Family Reunion Month, a young girl stopped at a halfway house in Rhode Island, filled out a postcard and mailed it to her family. Since they had not heard from her in three months, one can imagine how overjoyed they were to have word of her safety, even though they could not reach her or find out if she ever planned to return home. Just knowing that she was alive and safe would relieve them from sleepless nights when they imagined the worst.

SHELTERS AND OTHER COMMUNITY SERVICES

Many other organizations and individuals are working to help runaways so that they do not join the ranks of the permanently missing. Fourteen years ago, Covenant House, the nation's largest crisis shelter, began with the efforts of one man, Father Bruce Ritter, to help a group of ten children who had been forced to star in a pornographic movie in exchange for food and shelter. Many other shelter programs grew out of individual and community concerns.

Church groups, social service agencies, and concerned volunteers joined forces to form the National Network of Runaway and Youth Services, Inc., which now consists of more than 600 programs. They help to bring national attention to the needs of youth in crisis and to help communities to develop high quality, cost-effective programs to meet these needs.

For example, bus companies have joined forces with agencies that work with runaways in need of help. Grey-

Teenage volunteers confer with Dr. Fred Eckhardt, pastor of St. John's Evangelical Lutheran Church in New York City's Greenwich Village. The volunteers comb the streets for runaways in the hope of reaching them before they are hurt.

hound Lines, Inc., the intercity bus company, has posted billboards in twenty-seven major bus stations around the country listing the phone numbers of these agencies. Some bus companies will pay the bus fare for a runaway who wants to return home. The Travelers Aid Society in some cities helps runaways arrange for transportation home or to shelters. The New York Port Authority Youth Services Unit is made up of three police officers and three social workers who try to reach runaway children in the huge bus terminals of New York City before they become involved with "reception committees" that pretend to help but have their own special interests in mind.

In some cities, vans travel through the areas that attract runaways. For example, a van from Bridge Over Troubled Waters, a runaway shelter, drives through certain Boston streets offering free dental care, medical care, and drug therapy.

Although thousands of young people are being helped, many who need help never call the hotline. Far more support for the protection of such youth is desperately needed, and one can find such support coming from many fronts. Police departments, such as those in Lexington, Kentucky, and Los Angeles, California, have formed Sexually Exploited Child Units. In spite of the many cases in which police do not appear to be helpful in finding a person who has disappeared, many police and other law enforcement officials work overtime to help find a runaway who is missing.

New legislation permits the inclusion of runaways in the FBI's national computer network no matter how brief a time they have been missing. Such information may help to lower the number of runaways who are exploited, brutalized, and sometimes murdered.

CHAPTER 4

PARENTAL ABDUCTIONS

Hundreds of thousands of children are the unwilling victims of parents who kidnap them from the homes to which they are legally assigned. A mother may kidnap her children from their father, or a father may take his children and hide them from their mother.

The actual names given to the forceful separation of a child from a parent varies. It may be called legalized kidnapping, childnapping, child snatching, child stealing, or parental abduction. But no matter what the name, one parent suffers the trauma of a missing child and the child suffers, too.

CAUSES OF PARENTAL ABDUCTIONS

The reasons for parental abductions are varied, but almost all offenders think their actions are in the best interests of the child. For example, a father may believe that the mother of his children is abusing them. A mother may feel that the child will be better cared for with her than with the father. Other child stealers justify their acts by claiming that love drove them to steal their children from their former spouses. A refusal of visiting rights is sometimes the trigger for such desperate actions. Some parents kidnap children to spite their former partners or to keep them away from new step-parents.

Increasing Divorces:
Increasing Abductions
While no one knows exactly how may children are missing because of parental abduction, it seems certain that the number is increasing along with the number of divorces. Joint custody arrangements are still less common than the placing of children with one parent and arranging for limited visiting rights for the other. Many fathers are now playing an increasingly important role in the lives of their children and are more aware of the fact that divorcing a wife should not mean divorcing their children. Sometimes fathers are extremely dissatisfied with the custody arrangements worked out by judges, who usually rule in favor of the mother. Some are appealing for new rights through legal channels; but this procedure is expensive and often frustrating, and may be a factor in the increasing number of cases of child snatching by fathers who decide to take matters into their own hands.

On the other hand, child snatching is not always done by fathers. There are mothers who do not have custody of their children and who steal them, too. One support group for parental kidnap victims lists 35 percent male registrants.

All children are potential targets for parental abduction, but children whose parents are divorced or who are considering a separation are especially vulnerable. Many children are snatched from their home in one state and hidden in another. Even though states may have laws that approve the custody rights of a parent in a different state, these laws can be difficult to enforce and much time may go by before a child is returned home. When the parents who are contemplating a divorce come from different countries, the chance of one parent whisking a child away to his or her homeland without the permission of the other is high.

Studies that explore the problem of child snatching conclude that a child is most vulnerable to kidnapping before either parent has been awarded custody. At this time, no law is broken when one parent removes a child from the home of the other, even if that child is hidden so that no contact can be made by the other parent.

YOUNG CHILDREN ARE PRIME TARGETS

The prime targets for parental snatchers are children between the ages of three and eleven, with those between the ages of three and five the most likely victims. Children who are below the age of three create special problems for the abducting parent because they need such constant supervision, and children older than eleven are more likely to telephone home, alert law enforcement agencies, or manage to run away to the custodial parent than younger children.

PARENTAL DECEPTION AND DISTORTION

Some children who have been kidnapped by parents live in constant fear because of the lies they have been told in efforts to keep them from returning home. One father told his son that his mother was dangerous and would shoot them both if she found them. Telling a child that the other parent is unfit, or dead, is a popular tactic. Kidnapped children are often told by one parent that the other one has a new family and is not interested in having them back.

Nancy was kidnapped by her father when she was seven years old. Although she was not sure she believed him when he told her that her mother did not want her anymore, Nancy remembered the arguments between her parents when they all lived together. She thought of running away to her aunt's house, but then her mother and father would find her and start the awful fights again. She decided to stay with her father.

Some children who are stolen are so fearful of punishment by their kidnapping parent that they do not attempt to contact the custodial parent. Consider the plight of Bill. When Bill's father took him away, he considered calling his mother to tell her what had happened, but he did not have a chance to do so. His father kept him under twenty-four-hour surveillance. Even if he did manage to sneak a phone call, his father would eventually find out and beat him again.

PSYCHOLOGICAL IMPACT ON THE CHILD

The psychological impact of such experiences during and after the abduction is almost always extremely stressful for the child. During the episode, the child may experience fear of the abducting parent, grief over the loss of the other parent, guilt for not having contacted the other parent or having caused the conflicts between the parents in the first place, or feel that he or she has been discarded by the other parent and is no longer wanted. Fear, guilt, and loss of self-esteem result in confused feelings for the child about the parents and himself or herself, and may engender self-hate or hatred for the parents.

These experiences can leave children with lasting emotional scars, even if they are found and reunited with their custodial parent. Seeing themselves as pawns between their feuding parents, they have little chance of developing a feeling of trust, so crucial in the normal development of the child. When the people closest to them do not protect them at an age when they are dependent upon their parents for protection and support, they learn to view the world as a hostile place, where people cannot be trusted. Insecurity and fear may remain with them throughout their lives.

—34

A PARENT'S NIGHTMARE

Parents whose children are stolen from them by former mates may look endlessly without success. Not knowing where a child is, or whether a child is being abused, even though the caretaker is a parent, can be a nightmare for the parent whose child is missing. One father who kidnapped his son placed him with an uncle who neglected the boy. This father cared only about spiting his ex-wife by making her suffer the loss of the child.

One mother reports searching for her child day after day, wondering if every boy that she saw might be her son. Perhaps he had changed so much in three years that she would not recognize him if she stood next to him in a supermarket. Perhaps he would have changed so much that he would never want to return to the home they shared for many years. Many of the same problems plague fathers whose children are missing from their lives. The following case illustrates some of the realized fears and other problems encountered by both the victimized child and the parent.

Ruth was kidnapped by her father when she was eight years old. Although her father told her that her mother did not want to care for her anymore because she was marrying a man with several other children, Ruth wondered why she was never permitted to visit her mother. Each time she asked her father about this, he gave her a different answer and quickly changed the subject. Ruth thought about calling home, but her father had strict rules about using the phone. One time, with help from the operator, she did call her mother, and she found that her mother had been searching frantically for her. Together, Ruth and her mother arranged for her to escape from the father, to meet her mother secretly at a hospital crisis clinic and drive with her to her former home more than a thousand miles away. Ruth's mother was so afraid that they would be followed that she stopped at gas stations as seldom as possible. They never stopped at a restaurant, or relaxed until they were safely home. Once reunited at home,

Ruth's mother found it difficult to understand why she missed her father, the friends she had made while living with him, and the treasures she had left behind. Even though Ruth was glad to be home again, she continued to bear the effects of her experience. Her feelings about both parents remained confused, and she was torn between her allegiance to them and unsure where she belonged.

SEARCH FOR VICTIMS
OF PARENTAL ABDUCTION

The American Bar Association estimates that parents who lose their children through parental kidnapping have only three chances in ten of ever finding them. A group that champions children's rights predicted that unless children who are kidnapped by a parent are found within the first six months after their disappearance, they will be missing for years, or perhaps forever.

Legal help for these families varies from state to state, but it is seldom enough to satisfy the needs of the innocent people who need legal protection. Many custodial parents whose children are missing are pleading for help so that more attention will be paid to their problems.

■ *A Frustrating Experience*
Searching for missing children who have been abducted by a parent can be an ongoing frustrating experience. The Parental Kidnapping Prevention Act of 1980 was the first federal statute that was passed to make parental abduction a federal crime. The Lindbergh Act that was signed into federal law in 1932 was a strong reaction to the kidnapping of the Lindbergh baby by a stranger, although it excluded punishment for kidnapping by parents. The 1980 law, on the other hand, states that the Fugitive Felon Act applies to parental abductions when the kidnapper has fled the state or country to avoid prosecution if the state from which he or she has fled

makes the crime a felony. Since there is no uniform approach to parental kidnapping at the state level, the custodial parent has found herself or himself trapped in a legal maze in efforts to retrieve a missing child.

- *Parent Locator Service*
The Parental Kidnapping Act of 1980 allows states access to the Department of Health and Human Services' Federal Parent Locator Service. This data bank is not very useful since it stores information that may be outdated. Information from a person's tax returns or Social Security records that may be six to eighteen months old is not of much use to someone trying to track down a person who moves around frequently so as not to be caught. Furthermore, access to the Federal Parent Locator Service involves complicated procedures. Much the same is true of state locator systems. Dated information and information that is difficult to obtain can easily frustrate a parent under the stress of searching for a missing child.

If a parent locator service does find a child snatcher, the address and place of employment of the offender will be supplied, but the service will do no active searching. The parent of the missing child must proceed independently or go through court to retrieve the child.

- *Help from Friends*
  and the Community
Parents of missing children often learn of the whereabouts of the offending spouse through friends, in-laws, neighbors, business associates, and other acquaintances. By asking some of these people to have the abductor phone or write, they involve others in aiding them.

No matter what methods are used to locate the victim of a parental abduction, the search is usually difficult and often fruitless. Support systems for parents have sprung up in many communities in which parents whose children have been stolen help each other. Sometimes, such individuals or groups go beyond a local support system in their search for help.

- ### *The Birth of Child Find*

Such was the case with Gloria Yerkovich. In December 1974, Ms. Yerkovich was required by court order to let her six-year-old daughter Joanna visit her natural father. Since the child did not know her father, who had abandoned her shortly after birth, she was afraid to go with him when he came for her. The father carried the child in his arms to the car while she screamed in terror. What was supposed to be a short visit turned out to be a very long one, for Ms. Yerkovich did not see her child again for ten years.

In August 1984, Gloria Yerkovich and her daughter were reunited at the Ulster County Courthouse in New York. The reunion came after more than a month of legal negotiations between the Ulster County District Attorney, and attorneys for both of Joanna's parents. Under an agreement they reached, no charges were filed immediately against Franklin Pierce, Joanna's father. Gloria Yerkovich was given a year to decide whether to press charges against her husband.

Ms. Yerkovich's own grief over the loss of her abducted daughter, and the magnitude of the missing children problem led her to found Child Find, Inc., a national organization devoted to reuniting missing children and their parents. Child Find tries to reunite children and parents by making every possible effort to establish a two-way communication system. Rather than just following leads that may locate the missing child, the organization provides a means of helping a child find the parents.

For the children who have been stolen by their parents and told that their other parent no longer wants them, or that they have been given permission to take the child by the other parent, or that the other parent is dead, or some other story that leads the child to believe that he or she cannot go

Ivan Lee Hinton III
(Pell City, AL)
Born - 5/11/76
Abducted by father
6/14/79

Cynthia Lynn Sumpter
(Santa Clara, CA)
Born - 7/18/68
Abducted by stranger
4/27/74

FOUND

Anjeleeca M. Padmore
(El Paso, TX)
Born - 9/12/75
Abducted by mother
4/7/80

Jessica Laura Watts
(Lehigh, PA)
Born - 11/22/75
Abducted by mother
5/9/82

FOUND

Jeremy Clifford Long
(Los Angeles, CA)
Born - 3/27/81
Abducted by father
1/3/83

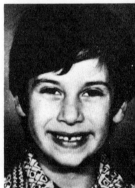

Cary Sayegh
(Clark, NV)
Born - 11/12/71
Abducted by stranger
10/25/78

Part of a poster distributed through the mail by Child Find, the national organization devoted to reuniting missing children with their families

home, Child Find provides a toll-free hotline. This hotline is available to any child searching for a parent as well as any concerned individual who can help identify a missing child.

Unfortunately, a parent who locates a missing child may still have a difficult time going through a legal maze in order to bring the child back. One organization that is trying to provide help for such parents and stolen children is the National Organization for Victim Assistance in Washington, D.C.

CHAPTER 5

STRANGER ABDUCTIONS

Of the many thousand youths who are reported missing each year, there are widespread estimates that from 6,000 to 50,000 are presumed to be victims of stranger abduction. Not many cases are solved, and an even smaller number of stranger-abducted children are recovered alive. These abductions often constitute the most heinous crimes, including sexual and other physical abuse, and murder.

WHO ARE CHILD ABDUCTORS?

According to the Federal Bureau of Investigation, their Behavioral Science Unit lists the following categories of stranger abductors:

pedophiles—people who are sexually attracted to children;

childless psychotics who have obsessive desires for a child;

profiteers—those who kidnap children with the intent

of using them in child pornography or who are black-market baby peddlers; and

"serial killers"—murderers who rove from state to state and often choose young people as their victims.

Pedophiles

The pedophiles constitute the largest number of predators of children. Often they are respected members of the community. Beneath their public facade lurk serious psychological disturbances that take the outward form of preying on children or adolescents. Sometimes the pedophile will abduct the victim for only a few hours or a day, or he may try to keep him indefinitely. In some cases, the tragic encounter may end in murder when the victim demands to be taken home. The following case is an example of an abduction by a pedophile.

Lenny was abducted at the age of seven by a man who lured him into his car on the pretext that he was going to drive him home to ask his mother for a church donation. Because Lenny had been punished by his father the day before, he believed his abductor (who learned of his punishment) when he told him his parents didn't want him anymore. Partly out of fear of the kidnapper, who sexually abused and beat him and kept him captive in his home, he gradually accepted the situation and did not attempt to run away. The man became both his daytime father and his nighttime sexual abuser. Despite his constant fear, Lenny settled into a semblance of family life as his abductor's son. His name was changed, he attended school, got Christmas and birthday presents, and made new friends.

When Lenny was fourteen, his "stepfather" brought home a new six-year-old boy to replace him, taunting Lenny that he was getting too old. It was fear and pity for the newly abducted child that brought Lenny to the local police station to charge his victimizer with kidnapping.

Lenny himself was reclaimed by his parents and his kidnapper was sentenced to jail. The experience has left lasting emotional scars on Lenny and the readjustment to his real family has been difficult and filled with turmoil for them all.

Childless Psychotics

Sometimes a child or baby is kidnapped to satisfy the needs of psychotic persons for a child. Usually this type of abduction involves a woman who cannot conceive a baby or has lost a child of her own, and seeks another to fill the maternal void. The following case illustrates such an abduction.

Denise Kay Gravely was two years old when she was abducted from her own yard where she was playing. A stranger, later discovered to be Charles Gress, took the little girl about 150 miles from her home, across state lines, to the home of his mother, Mrs. Schmidt. This woman's daughter had died at birth many years earlier, but she still talked constantly of wanting a daughter. Evidently, her son thought he could fill her need by presenting Denise to his mother and telling her that she was his own child. Although it seems likely that Mrs. Schmidt was always aware of the fact that Denise was not really her granddaughter, she cared for the child for a period of 19 months. Then her joy was shattered.

Donald Gress, the brother of the kidnapper, was a friend of Denise's father who had helped him distribute fliers after her disappearance. The father appeared on many television programs appealing for the safe return of his daughter, and Donald Gress shared his grief. Nineteen months passed after the child's disappearance before Donald Gress discovered the child at his own mother's home. Donald Gress reported the case to the police, who located the child at the Schmidt home and returned her to her family.

Profiteers

Child pornography has developed into a highly organized multi-million-dollar industry with operations on a nationwide

scale. Although many adolescents and teenagers become involved in these operations after running away from home, many children are forcibly abducted by profiteers who are interested in using them in pornographic films or photographs. Many of these children and teenagers disappear after their roles are finished. Many become involved in sex rings that expolit teenagers and children for prostitution.

In addition, kiddie porn may often be responsible for further abductions by pedophiles. Kristin Cole Brown, Information Director of Child Find, Inc., believes that kiddie porn readers may be directly incited to abduct and rape a child. She stresses the need for greater cooperation among law enforcement agencies, community leaders, parents, and other concerned people to put a stop to the sexual exploitation of our youth.

Another type of profiteer is the criminal who abducts babies or children for the purpose of selling them illegally in black-market adoptions. Still another type of kidnapper is one who abducts a child for ransom, but far fewer of these kidnappings have occurred in recent years.

Serial Murderers
The serial murderer is a relatively new breed of killer who roves from one state to another killing one victim after another. Many serial murderers select a particular category of victim, and since children are vulnerable, they are often singled out. When police investigators in one state begin to follow clues leading to the murderer, he moves to another state. He

Wayne Williams, convicted in Georgia for the slaying of Nathaniel Cater, and the possible murderer of twenty-seven other children and teenagers in Atlanta, is shown here, handcuffed and on his way to court.

seldom knows his victims before he seizes them, but a category such as children, women, migrant workers, or homosexuals is the target for his inner rage.

NEED FOR PREVENTIVE MEASURES

Many communities have introduced programs to educate their children about stranger abduction and the precautions that they can take. Some people have the mistaken attitude that nothing will ever happen to their children, so they avoid discussing with their children what kinds of lures are used by these abductors. Many parents think they need only tell their children not to take candy from strangers. These same people instruct their children about the dangers of fire escapes, the availability of poison centers, or the need for traffic safety, or seat belts in cars. Perhaps they do not realize that giving children preventive information that will protect them from abduction can be done in a manner that will not unduly scare them.

Child kidnappers are often crafty in their use of lures to encourage children and young people to go with them peacefully. No matter what your age, knowing about these lures and spreading such information to the younger children in your family or community can help to prevent tragedy. New programs that teach precautions against stranger abduction make it clear that most adults care about the protection of children and only a very small percentage of them prey on children. They stress caution of strangers without fear.

There are many ways to illustrate lures without unduly frightening children. One example is the telling of a story such as the following:

Twelve-year-old Paul had been warned about talking to strangers, but that was about all his family felt he should know about the frightening subject of child abduction. He never noticed the man who watched him practice soccer on Thursday afternoons. He had just joined the team that would represent his city in the national playoff in Florida. He was very excited about traveling with the team and having his family join him for a week in Florida in the middle of winter. Paul's team membership entitled him to three passes on the plane that was being chartered for the team. This would mean that his family, who hated the cold winters at home, would have a vacation that they could not normally afford. Tina, his sister, was so proud of him that she could not stop talking to her friends about her wonderful brother.

As Paul walked home after the practice one Thursday, he was dreaming of the Florida game. The man who had been watching him stopped his car and asked for directions. He told Paul that he was looking for the house where he used to live just to see it once more before he went back to his present home. He explained that he had not seen his birthplace for many years and the neighborhood had changed so much that he was lost. Paul directed the man to the proper street and was about to continue on his way when the stranger asked if he knew the Rogers family. He described them as former neighbors and Paul was pleased to find that they both knew Bill Rogers. Paul had no way of knowing that the name Rogers was one that the man had selected because it was the name on the local hardware store. There was a good chance that the store owner lived in the town and that Paul would know him. Paul unwittingly had provided a first name, and it was easy to use this information as a means of being friendly.

During the conversation, the driver of the car told Paul that he had hurt his arm playing soccer, and he also apologized for the mess in his car, which consisted of some athletic clothing strewn about and a soccer ball on the floor. Paul chatted with his new acquaintance about the game that was so important in his life. When he was offered a lift, he felt very comfortable about getting into the car. He used to hitchhike almost everywhere, but he had stopped after one of his friends had a bad experience. However, this man was a friend of Bill Rogers, and he used to live several blocks from

Paul's house. Besides, Paul was tired after the practice. It would be good to have a ride home with someone who appreciated soccer.

Unfortunately, Paul never reached home. The injured arm became stronger when they reached an intersection that led to the woods at the edge of town. Paul's protests about taking the wrong road were soon muffled by a blow to his head. He never played in the Florida game, but he watched it from a hospital bed. He felt fortunate to be alive after a harrowing experience that ended when he escaped from his captor and managed to attract the attention of a passerby with his screams.

This story illustrates just one of the many common lures used by child abductors. The National Child Safety Council points out that abductors usually target a victim ahead of time, picking a child or adolescent whom they think will be an easy touch. Be sure that you and the younger members of your family are aware of the many subterfuges used by abductors.

COMMON LURES USED BY CHILD ABDUCTORS

1. Asking for directions is one of the most common lures that is used by people who abduct boys and girls. Although most children have learned at an early age not to talk to strangers, many are tricked into feeling that the strangers are really friends.

2. Asking for various kinds of help is often used by people to lure children into places where they can be exploited. A common appeal of child abductors is to ask a child to help find their pet, a request a child finds difficult to refuse. "Help me find my dog" is often followed by a detour to the woods.

3. "Your mother is hurt and she has asked me to take you to her at once," says the kindly stranger. This kind of trick can be eliminated by the use of a code word. Many parents are

telling their children not to go with anyone under such circumstances unless they are asked for a code word and can reply with the one agreed upon by the family. Any word can serve this purpose as long as it is not so common that the offender might happen to guess it.

4. Although abductors can use any kind of transportation to trap a child, or even operate without a vehicle, experts suggest that children should be especially cautious about the drivers of vans.

Sandra was trying to be helpful when a man who said he was having trouble with his van asked her to turn the key in the ignition so he could watch what was happening under the hood. As she stepped into the driver's seat, a man who was hiding in the van grabbed her and pulled her in the back.

5. A request for assistance with a car problem of any nature is often followed by a request that the helper go along to the gas station or get into the car for some other reason. The safest way to deal with such a request is by going to a pay phone or one in a familiar home and calling a gas station, garage, or whatever place can supply the help.

6. Most children are warned about not allowing strangers to enter their homes or to let anyone know that they are alone there. Telling someone who calls on the phone that their mother or father is in the shower or too busy to come to the phone is less difficult than resisting a person who comes to the door showing a badge. Police badges and other badges are easily imitated. A real policeman will not object to a child's contacting a neighbor to help in any stated emergency. For example, if the badge holder requests that a child go to the hospital because a parent is injured, a neighbor can be called to verify the situation.

7. Since most children have been carefully taught to respect authority figures such as teachers, policemen, firemen, truant officers, and clergy, assailants can make use of this

respect by impersonating such a figure. Children should be taught to ask another adult or neighbor to check a person's credentials before going along with them.

A policeman or other person may accuse a child of wrongdoing when he or she is innocent. For example, a person posing as a store detective might accuse a child of stealing something and insist that the child come along to the office. Asking for the help of a nearby adult is recommended in such a case.

8. Kevin was tricked by a young man who joined the baseball game on the lot near his house. He was a good player and Kevin enjoyed the help he gave him with his batting problems. After the game was over, Kevin was proud to be asked to ride home with his new friend. Sometimes this kind of situation can be completely innocent, but it is wise to consider such a new acquaintance as a stranger.

9. Pretending to be disabled or not to speak the native language is a popular way of disarming a child. Asking an adult to help, or just refusing to help if no other adult is nearby, is the sensible thing to do.

10. Tim and Mary were warned many times about going with strangers who offered candy, toys, rewards, and other kinds of bribes for doing work at their homes. However, they had never heard of the lure that is an appeal to vanity through promises of modeling jobs, beauty contest participation, a place on an athletic team, or opportunities to star in a commercial. Fortunately, Tim and Mary used quick thinking and refused to accept the offer of a man who promised to take their pictures for a magazine in a secret film session. When they suggested that he call their parents, the man was no longer interested in them.

Make it clear to children that one can be house wise and street wise by remembering that adults who really want help usually ask another adult. Although only about 20 percent of all children will ever be approached by anyone who has bad intentions, it is wise to avoid being alone in places that are favorite hunting spots of such people. These places include short cuts from school, lonely streets, isolated parks and school grounds, or any place that is far from the eyes of others. Use the buddy system when you have to use a bathroom in a public place such as the movies, and try to use well-traveled areas.

CHILD SAFETY FAIRS

One exciting new and wide-reaching attempt to educate parents and children on the problem of stranger abduction and the need to protect themselves is the introduction of Child Safety Fairs. These fairs are increasing throughout the United States and are being sponsored by ACTION, the United States Department of Justice and the American Association of Retired Persons. The first Child Safety Fairs began in the spring of 1984. Some were held on successive weekends and others were held as a single day seminar. Volunteers who run the fairs have recorded the height, weight, and distinguishing characteristics of the children who attended and took their photographs and fingerprints. The numbers of children processed at these fairs are impressive, with as many as 3,000 children attending a one-day fair.

As these Child Safety Fairs have spread throughout the country, they have promoted an awareness of the whole problem of missing children. Even though the fairs emphasize the gathering of information, most sponsors and volunteers feel that their most important contribution is the education of the public about the need to protect children from stranger abduction. A handbook that gives directions for sponsoring a Child Safety Fair suggests that the participation of a parent and child together, in such a safety program, produces a special bond of prevention, protection, and understanding.

HOW YOUNG ADULTS CAN HELP

Young adults can play an important role in helping to prevent stranger abduction by taking part in programs such as Child Safety Fairs as well as encouraging adults to hold them. Numerous public and private organizations have come together to provide support and guidance to groups wishing to hold Child Safety Fairs and to follow up with community-wide child protection efforts. Organizations that are eager to assist in such projects are listed on pages 97-98. To obtain further information, contact ACTION at the address listed there.

You may wish to list lures in your school newspapers or encourage parent groups to learn about them and educate their children. Here is a list of safety rules that could be printed and distributed to elementary and junior high school children. It includes many of the safety rules that have been compiled by the Child Safety Fair Committee:

SAFETY RULES FOR CHILDREN

Learn your full name, address, and telephone number, including area code. (Many children have been frustrated in attempts to find parents because they did not know an area code.)

- Learn how to dial 911 in case of emergency.

- Always phone home to tell parents where you are, especially if your plans have changed.

Soap opera star Ruth Warrick and Eevin Hartsrugh from the television show "All My Children" display Eevin's poster for a contest championing National Missing Children's Day, May 25th. The theme of the contest is "Children's Safety."

- Avoid strangers and be aware that someone known only by sight may not be a friend.

- Do not mistake a person who delivers a package to your house for a family friend.

- If you are being followed by someone in a car or on foot, run to other people or to a well-lit place. Do not hide in the bushes.

- Never approach an adult in a car even if the adult signals to you.

- Tell the delivery man to leave his package at the door by talking to him through a window.

- Try to go places with a friend.

- Avoid parking lots, dark places, and abandoned places.

- Scream "help" if you are in trouble.

- If you are grabbed by anyone, scream "help," kick, and attempt to break loose.

- Ask to not be left alone in a car by anyone who drives you anywhere. If you are left alone, roll up the windows of the car so that only enough space is left at the top of the glass to put a finger through. If a stranger approaches the car, blow the horn and continue to blow it until help arrives.

- Be aware that a person who sees your name on a shirt or hears another person use it could pretend to know you.

Although there are so many different kinds of lures used by people who abduct children that one might think the problem is hopeless, awareness of the common ones, quick thinking, and preventive education can play an important part in preventing tragedy.

CHAPTER 6
PRECAUTIONS: THE ISSUE OF FINGERPRINTING AND RECORD KEEPING

Although everyone agrees that something needs to be done to make it easier to search for missing children, there is little agreement on how to go about doing it. Senator Paul Simon introduced legislation in Congress to establish a hotline for information about missing children and to provide funds for research on the problem. In his exploration of the dilemma, he noted that there were usually two basic obstacles: the searches were launched too late and they were doomed because there was too little information.

RECORD KEEPING OF CHILDREN URGED

Parents in many communities are being urged to keep records of their children just in case the child disappears. Records of height, weight, eye color, skin color, identifying marks, and recent photographs can be helpful for every member of a family. One of the more controversial items suggested for a complete record of children and teenagers is fingerprints. Those who argue for fingerprint programs in schools point out that it is necessary because most children have not established themselves with a personal history. Adults have the benefit, on the other hand, of such identification as Social Security numbers, driver's licenses, car titles, bank accounts, credit cards, and real estate titles.

Fingerprints are considered to be one of the most effective tools for positive identification of children. In addition to fingerprints, other records that can help to identify children include blood type, birthmarks, scars, and current photographs. Younger children should be photographed frequently, so that a recent picture is always available.

Ideally, parents should keep records of their children in a place where they are safe but easily available. If a child disappears on a Friday night, records in their safe deposit box will probably not be available until Monday morning. Even a two-day delay can be too long a period of time to trace the tracks of an abducted child. Since children change so rapidly, updating all records is important. The family of six-year-old Danny regretted their lack of records.

Danny disappeared one summer afternoon when he wandered into the woods near his home. Posters and newspapers carried his description far and wide. Twelve hundred people helped in the search, combing hundreds of acres of thick woods and marshy terrain near the trailer park where he lived with his parents. Their search continued for weeks after he disappeared. Danny's family pleaded for his safe return through posters, letters to newspapers, and television appearances. They continued to tell themselves that most children who are missing are found sooner or later, but as time passed, their hopes faded. The only records of Danny were photographs taken shortly before he disappeared. Their value faded with time.

One day, there was a telephone call from the police in a city about fifty miles from where Danny lived. Although this came almost two years after his disappearance, the boy who was brought to them just might be Danny. Would his parents come to see if this might be their child? What a foolish question! They would be there as fast as possible.

Danny's father kept telling his wife not to be too hopeful, and he told himself the same thing. Both parents could not help but feel that this must be their child. Unfortunately, it was not. This was not the first time they had been disappointed. Each time an unidentified child that vaguely fit Danny's description was listed at a police station within miles around, Danny's parents checked to see if that child might be their missing son.

One report of a child who was found with a group of wandering gypsies gave Danny's parents more hope than they had ever had with any of the previous clues. The photographs of the child that were sent to them by the police had a strong resemblance to the Danny they knew. They knew that he would have changed in the years that had passed, but he might well have looked like the child in the pictures. The boy's hair was darker than Danny's, but his hair could have grown darker as he grew older. The chin was much the same as that of their son. So were the shape of his eyes and the lines of his nose. Or did they just hope these features were the same as Danny's?

After visiting the boy who might have been Danny, his parents were disappointed once more. Somehow, they knew that this was not their child. But was there a chance that it might have been? They would continue to search for years to come. And they would blame themselves many times for not participating in the system of fingerprinting that was used in some schools. Even though no one had suggested this at Danny's school, the parents felt that somehow they should have known to keep records of his fingerprints. No matter how often people told them they were not to blame, Danny's parents felt guilty about his disappearance.

SCHOOL FINGERPRINTING PROGRAMS: A CONTROVERSIAL ISSUE

Most parents readily give their permission in a school fingerprinting program. Some, realizing that it is unlikely that such information will ever be needed, still feel that a fingerprint record is a good thing to have on file. But many individuals, including some who are not parents, object to fingerprinting programs for a variety of reasons, most frequently having to do with civil liberties. The following are some of the questions being asked.

■ *Objections to*
Fingerprinting Children
Might fingerprinting scare the children? Young children might think that they have done something wrong and are being fingerprinted much the way criminals are on television shows. Perhaps something they did in the last few days seems important to the child. Is the fingerprinting necessary because Sam hit his sister?

Might fingerprints reach the wrong hands and someday be used against a child in a criminal investigation? The schools promise to give the only set of prints to the parents, but there are some people who do not trust them or their intentions.

Will fingerprinting frighten children about abduction un-necessarily? Most young children report that the process is fun. Five-year-old Molly said fingerprinting was somewhat like fingerpainting. Kim and Lisa reported that it tickled when they rolled their fingers on the ink and the paper. Four-year-old Amy assured others that it did not even hurt when the lady rubbed the ink from her fingers after she pressed it on the paper.

Some older children who have participated in fingerprint-ing programs express concern about the need for such action. Volunteer workers who administer the program are quick to explain that the chances that the fingerprints will ever be needed are extremely slight. But many young people find comfort in the fact that their parents will have a record in case of an emergency.

One of the arguments against fingerprinting is that par-ents may have a false feeling of security after participating in a program. Fingerprinting may be counterproductive if parents feel that such a program will really do the job of protecting their child and that they do not need to do anything more.

Will fingerprinting of children help to deter strangers from kidnapping children? Although people in favor of the programs hope that it may help to do so, many think the idea is unrealistic.

There is disagreement as to whether fingerprinting is of any value in cases of parental kidnappings. Although it may not prevent an estranged parent from snatching a child, it might help in locating a child who is using a false name and has come under suspicion of not being the person a parent claims the child to be.

- *Proponents of
  Fingerprinting Programs*
  In spite of the voices that are raised in protest, fingerprinting is winning the approval of many organizations. It has the support of state and local police, the Federal Bureau of Investigation, church groups, civic groups, and most parents.

One citizen action group that is concerned with the problem of missing children, the Cobra Connection, recommends that mandatory fingerprinting of every child is needed at birth to help prevent child kidnapping and to increase the possibility of locating children who are missing. They point out that parents do not object to having baby footprints made in the hospital so that babies will not be mixed and given to the wrong parent. A palm print could be taken at the same time and the records of both the footprint and palmprint could be kept in a safe place by the parents.

The nation's first statewide children's identification program began in Washington State in July of 1984. Children can be fingerprinted and photographed for driver's license-type identification cards at any office in the state that issues driver's licenses. The fee is nominal and updates of the identification can be made for just one dollar. Copies of finger-

prints and photos will be kept by the state, and if a child is ever missing, the information can be released by parents to the authorities.

In announcing the program, Governor John Spellman said, "This is no police state." He said that the program was needed to fight "the heartbreak and tragedy of missing children." He made it clear that the program is strictly voluntary, and the information will only be used if the parent agrees to its release.

The National Children's Fingerprint Bank in Sarasota, Florida has released information to the press that it will safely file the fingerprints of any child for a period of ten years at a small fee. This organization promises to make the fingerprints available to recognized authorities twenty-four hours a day, seven days a week.

Many communities make the fingerprinting of children available through their police departments. Some of these programs are at a local level, while others are large scale. For example, the Exploited and Missing Child Unit of Jefferson County, Kentucky, was formed in July 1980 to assist parents of missing children and to help children who are sexually exploited. A study indicated that over 86 percent of youth involved in child prostitution/pornography in Jefferson County were runaway or missing children at the time of those acts. As a result of this study, a project to fingerprint all of the children in the country was implemented.

Even though the chances of a child's disappearing are very slight, the horror of such a thing makes many parents eager to participate in any fingerprinting program and to

A brother and sister are among the first schoolchildren to be fingerprinted by a policeman in the village of Buffalo Grove, Illinois.

make records of their children that would help in the search for a missing child.

PUBLIC AWARENESS: A MUST FOR PREVENTION

More work toward prevention, further public awareness, education, and action is strongly needed. For example, fingerprinting will do little to stop children from running away, the most common cause of their disappearance. More attention needs to be paid to strengthening family relationships. Many community activists feel, however, that an emphasis on the importance of record keeping can help in promoting awareness of the whole missing children problem.

CHAPTER 7

THE GRASS ROOTS MOVEMENT

For many years, the following pattern of concern about missing children was typical. The report of a missing child reached the newspapers and television screens of the nation, and people raised their voices about this alarming problem. Then, most of the public continued with their own daily lives and soon forgot the tragedy that seemed so real and horrible when they first learned about it. However, in many of the neighborhoods where a child or young person was found missing, groups of volunteers gathered to help in the search, to inform the public about the magnitude of the problem, to press for better nationwide cooperation, and to continue to alert their lawmakers to the missing children problem.

For many of the families, friends, and others who had some personal involvement, improving the means of searching for missing children and young people became the single most important cause in their lives. It is largely through their efforts that public awareness and increased action developed to cope with this problem. Today, few would disagree that the victimization of children is among the saddest facts of life in our society.

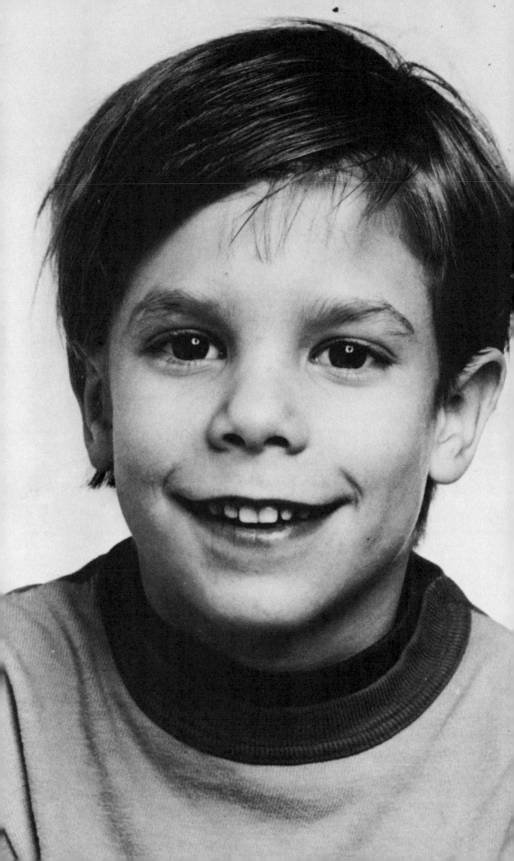

THE CASE OF ETAN PATZ

Perhaps the most famous missing child in the United States is Etan Patz, whose case is credited with bringing the first large-scale attention to the problem of missing children. Many people empathize with the feelings of the parents of this six-year-old boy who kissed his mother goodbye on the morning of May 25, 1979 and began the two-block walk to the place where he would catch the bus for his first-grade class at Public School 3 in New York City. Etan never reached the school bus stop that day. His disappearance set off one of the most extensive manhunts in the history of New York. But after years of active searching and thousands of leads, there is not a shred of solid evidence as to what happened to this boy. His parents have never been able to learn if he is alive or dead.

The anguish that the Patzes have suffered began with a simple observance that he was very late in coming home from school. Suppose they had been made aware of their son's disappearance early in the morning of that first day. Chances of finding him would have been much greater.

In addition to searching for their own child, the parents of Etan Patz have been instrumental in developing further interest in the problem and in spearheading increased action to locate other children who disappear.

THE DEVELOPMENT OF ACTION

ACTION, a national network of agencies that works for increased aid in the search for missing people, was formed

Etan Patz's disappearance from his neighborhood in New York set off one of the most extensive searches in the city's history.

by the parents of Etan Patz. The organization was later led by John Clinkscales, whose son, Kyle, disappeared in 1976. This college student had visited his family on Tuesday, January 27th, left some clothes to be washed, and said that he would be back on Friday. The book, *Kyle's Story: Friday Never Came,* was written by his father to help others search for missing children and teens, and describes the experiences of the Clinkscales in searching for their only son. Mr. Clinkscales notes that he soon became aware that the family of a missing person must depend largely on its own initiative and ingenuity.

The name ACTION stands for "A Confederation To Inform Others Nationally." Its purposes are to promote awareness about the magnitude of the problem of missing children, to provide information for families who are among the victims, to urge lawmakers to give needed legislation and law enforcement personnel to give missing children cases a higher priority, and to encourage the missing to contact their families even if they wish to keep their whereabouts secret.

LOCAL PROGRAM BECOMES NATIONWIDE ORGANIZATION

Many other fledgling programs have been started locally by the families of missing children and some have grown within a few years into nationwide organizations. For example, the Dee Scofield Awareness Program was born in September 1976, several months after the disappearance of twelve-year-old Dee Scofield from an Ocala, Florida, shopping center. The program began with an article that was placed in a church paper. Copies of the article were sent to family members who were scattered around the country, and they were urged to place it in their local papers. In a few years, the program grew so widespread that the organization was able to assist several hundred families and missing children from more than thirty states.

A DIRECTORY
OF MISSING CHILDREN

Some organizations spread information about missing children through their publications. For example, Child Find, Inc., includes a physical description of each child that is registered with the organization in the Child Find's Directory of Missing Children. The Directory is distributed to police departments, schools, and other institutions across the country.

THE TRAGEDY OF ADAM WALSH

More than fifty million people have heard of the tragedy of Adam Walsh, the six-year-old boy whose story was told in the television movie that was produced by Linda Otto. This media event, in which Adam's parents offered their full cooperation, was part of a crusade against the abuse and exploitation of children. The commitment of Reve and John Walsh toward putting an end to the suffering of abduction victims has spearheaded important action.

The tragedy of Adam Walsh began on July 27, 1981. Adam was permitted to wait for his mother in the toy department of a Florida store while she looked at lamps just three aisles away. In the few minutes before Adam's mother went to join him, he disappeared. When she could not find Adam, Mrs. Walsh set in motion the paging systems both inside the store and outside the store in the mall. When there was no response, she called the police. Adam's father rushed to the mall, where both parents were questioned about the boy's habits by the police. They assured the police that their child would not wander off by himself or go home alone.

The search for Adam Walsh continued throughout the day and night. A recent photograph and full description of the child were given to the police and local television stations. A reward was offered for his return. Posters were placed in strategic places and scores of volunteers searched the neighborhood. The police wired other departments in the state, but when morning came, Adam was still missing.

Adam's parents appeared on television the morning following his disappearance pleading for more help from the community. They also gave personal directions to their son that might help him find his way home, using familiar landmarks that they had taught him.

Imagine the dismay of Mr. Walsh when he contacted the Federal Bureau of Investigation and discovered that they would not become involved in the case unless there was further evidence of a kidnapping in the form of a ransom note or specific evidence that the child was taken out of the state. And imagine the frustration these parents must have felt when they learned that a policewoman who called another jurisdiction in Florida was told that they could not look for Adam because their case loads were too heavy.

Adam never followed the directions his parents gave him on the local television show. He could not. Shortly before Reve and John Walsh appeared on a national program in New York to appeal for help in finding their son, they learned that the remains of a boy had been found in a Florida canal. Later, dental records confirmed that the remains were Adam's.

ADAM WALSH CHILD RESOURCE CENTER

In order to share with others what they had learned from their experience, the Walshes contributed much of their time and energy to promoting children's issues. Child Advocacy, Inc., a nonprofit corporation that had been working for missing, abused, and neglected children since 1973, changed its name to the Adam Walsh Child Resource Center and continues to work toward improving the lot of children through a variety of techniques including public awareness, education of children and adults, coalition building, statute revision, and research. The Walshes have repeatedly testified before Con-

A moment of triumph for John, Reve, and Meghan Walsh,
the family of Adam Walsh, when President Ronald Reagan
signed the Missing Children Act on October 12, 1982

gressional committees and have traveled around the country mobilizing national support for the increased protection of children. Their testimony, along with that of others, played a large part in the passage of the Missing Children Act of 1982, described in Chapter One. In fact, John Walsh has been called the spokesman for all missing children.

EFFORTS OF THE MEDIA

Although many efforts to find missing children are initiated by parents whose children have disappeared, investigative reporters and film producers sometimes become heavily involved. Linda Otto, who produced the documentary for television as well as the movie, *Adam,* founded an organization, Find the Children. This nonprofit organization has objectives that are as diverse as the problem itself. They include

1. distributing funds raised by the foundation to other nonprofit organizations concerned with missing children;

2. promoting greater federal involvement and state cooperation in recovering missing children;

3. coordinating the production of public service announcements for local, regional, and national nonprofit search organizations;

4. lobbying national and local media to broadcast and publish, as a regular format, pictures and descriptions of missing children;

5. establishing a monetary reward system for information leading to the arrest and conviction in stranger-abduction cases.

AGENCIES WORK TOGETHER

Many self-help agencies continue to struggle to reach large numbers of people in spite of their small budgets. They sponsor fund-raising events, use volunteer help and contributions, and distribute newsletters of their activities. Some of the organizations work together. For example, Dee Scofield Awareness Program, Find-Me, Inc., Missing Teens and Young Adults, National Missing Children's Locate Center, Edwin Shaw IV, and the Society for Young Victims have joined in sponsoring Family Reunion Month, mentioned in an earlier chapter.

Even though new laws to help in the search for missing children are beginning to appear at local and national levels, much work remains to be done. Private groups, both large and small, will continue to provide valuable help for those who suffer the tragedy of missing children.

CHAPTER 8

TOWARD A
SAFER FUTURE

Action by governmental agencies and legislation to help prevent the disappearance of children and to track those who are missing is on the upswing.

NATIONAL CRIME
INFORMATION CENTER

The earliest federal involvement came after testimony from parents of missing children; pressure from concerned members of Congress led to the passage of the Missing Children Act in 1982 described in Chapter One. This milestone legislation essentially accomplished two things. First, it encourages law enforcement agencies to enter missing children and young people into the National Crime Information Center computer. It also permits parents to register a child if law enforcement agencies fail to do so.

Secondly, the Act mandated that coroners' offices throughout the United States report information about unidentified bodies to the FBI. Each year in the United States from 2,000 to 5,000 individuals are buried as John or Jane Doe and many of these bodies are those of children. For

A computer bank with information about missing children at the FBI National Crime Information Center

those who search for a child year after year, finding that their child is dead is horrible indeed, but it can at least end the agony of fruitless searching and not knowing if a missing child is alive or dead.

Certainly, a computer bank that stores the names, dates of birth, physical characteristics, and circumstances of disappearances increases the chances of finding a child quickly. But the federal system is a new system, and it is possible that many law enforcement agencies do not use it. Senator Paula Hawkins, one of the leading sponsors of the legislation that resulted in the Missing Children Act, has suggested guidelines for parents attempting to include their children in the clearinghouse. These may be obtained through Child Find or the Missing Children Project of the National Organization for Victim Assistance (NOVA).

Although any child or young person, whether a runaway or a victim of parental or stranger abduction, is eligible for inclusion in the National Crime Information Center missing persons file, this system is just a clearinghouse of information. The Act only makes the system available. It does not put into action any search for the individual. To mandate its use, each state must pass its own Missing Children Act.

THE NATIONAL CENTER FOR MISSING AND EXPLOITED CHILDREN

In 1984, the United States Government set up The National Center for Missing and Exploited Children to help parents find their missing children and to educate parents and law enforcement agencies to prevent exploitation of children and teens. A toll-free hotline is available to collect reports of sightings of missing children. There is also a technical staff of former law enforcement professionals who are experienced in the handling of missing children cases who provide counsel for the families. Tips from callers are turned over to local authorities and to the Federal Bureau of Investigation.

The newly formed National Center for Missing and Exploited Children includes a division for missing children, a division for exploited children, and a division for education, prevention, and public awareness. The Missing Children Division actively assists individuals and agencies by providing sophisticated information on searching techniques, effectively distributing and viewing pictures of missing children in the media and nationally coordinating and assisting the network of nonprofit citizen groups who are addressing the issue. The Division for Exploited Children provides national coordination between registered missing children and those who have been reported to have been criminally assaulted during their absence from home. This division also provides technical assistance to law enforcement agencies, the criminal justice system, and state and local agencies in the investigation of child exploitation cases. The Division of Education, Prevention, and Public Awareness collects and disseminates the most effective programs to be used by home, school, and the community for the purposes of education and prevention.

One of the important aims of the center is to effect permanent change by providing a national clearinghouse of information on effective state and federal legislation directed at the protection of children and the reduction of child victimization. Every searching parent and law enforcement agency can obtain technical assistance packets on effective searching techniques from the National Center on Missing and Exploited Children. A national directory of nonprofit citizen organizations is available from the center, too.

THE NATIONAL CHILD VICTIM NETWORK: A PUBLIC SERVICE

Another new program, the National Child Victim Network is largely the result of the efforts of Kenneth Wooden, an author and investigative reporter. This nationwide, computerized program to trace missing children and the suspects who prey on them began many years ago with Kenneth Wooden's concern for the need of a tool to help track down the murderers of children. Mr. Wooden's work in the field of children's rights led to the founding of the National Coalition for Children's Justice in 1976. This group gained the respect and support of many influential individuals. The current chairman of the Board of Trustees of the organization is George Gallup, Jr., president of the Gallup Poll and son of its founder. The development of the National Child Victim Network has been aided by private financing from a number of endowments and social programs of large corporations.

The network is designed to involve the police departments of about twenty-six cities with major airports where there is a heavy trade in abducted children. Information about these activities was gained through years of interviewing those involved in criminal actions. The network is built around the major metropolitan areas where missing children are most likely to be found. It aims to track abductors who criss-cross state lines and the underground networks that now operate regionally and nationally with near impunity.

The Coalition Network allows police investigators of different jurisdictions to gather, process, and share information on specific missing and murdered children. It leaves control of all investigations in local hands, and allows each local department to determine the nature and extent of its own participation. The network protects the privacy of individual citizens while increasing the ability of local police departments to rapidly analyze the important information pertaining to a case, with computer programs designed specifically for police investigators' methods and thought patterns. It is also designed to continue active research in the patterns of runaways and organized rings that abduct, sell, and generally prey on children.

There are over 16,000 police departments in the United States and each is under local jurisdiction. Suppose a girl is abducted from a city on the East Coast and sold to a pimp who operates on the West Coast, where she is murdered. She may have been reported missing in the region from which she was abducted, but police in the city thousands of miles away may be totally unaware of this report. This is just one of the areas in which the network can improve the difficult task of tracking missing children. Further information about this network can be found in *Prey: Missing and Murdered Children*, a book that is the product of five years of investigative research by its author, Kenneth Wooden.

LEGISLATION TO COMBAT SEXUAL ABUSE OF CHILDREN

Increased public and professional concern over the exploitation and sexual abuse of children and teens for commercial gain, and the disappearance of many of these youths because of this exploitation, resulted in two important developments in 1982. One was the investigation and report of the U.S. General Accounting Office on teenage prostitution and child pornography and on the efforts of the government to deal with these problems. The second was a decision by the U.S. Supreme Court that unanimously confirmed the constitutionality of state laws that prohibit the dissemination of material depicting children engaged in sexual conduct regardless of whether or not the material is obscene.

These actions did not put an end to the sexual exploitation of children through pornography, but they paved the way for minimizing the problem. Although some states have strong laws, this is not true of all. And there is always the problem of how well the laws are enforced.

In an effort to attack this problem, Congress enacted the Protection of Children Against Sexual Exploitation Act in 1978. In addition to extending the federal government's authority to prosecute the producers and distributers of child pornography, it prohibits the transportation of all children across state lines for the purpose of sexual exploitation. Formerly, only girls were protected from transportation across state lines.

The Sexual Exploitation of Children Act of 1983 was introduced after Congress found that child pornography had developed into a highly organized multi-million-dollar industry with operations on a nationwide scale. This Act strengthened the earlier one from 1978, but it certainly was not the whole answer to the problem.

The Center Against Sexual Assault in Phoenix, Arizona, and other concerned individuals have expressed great concern about the number of children who appear in X-rated movies. While some action has been taken to prevent children from seeing such movies, more action is needed for the unfortunate children who act in them. Many children and young teenagers disappear after their roles are finished.

PROGRAM TO TRACK SEX OFFENDERS

A recently developed project that is helping to protect such children and retrieve those who have been abducted is known as the National Missing/Abducted Children and Serial Murder Tracking and Prevention Program and commonly called MACSMTP. In a number of planning sessions, experts gathered to lay the groundwork for a nationwide system to trace missing or abducted children and adults, to track and apprehend "serial murderers," and to explore the links between sexual abuse and delinquency. They dealt with the subjects of child pornography, child prostitution, and juvenile delinquency resulting from sexual abuse and the exploitation of children. This knowledge is being integrated into the Violent Criminal Apprehension Program (VICAP).

THE FEDERAL BUREAU OF INVESTIGATION GETS INVOLVED

After three years of planning, the system referred to as VICAP began operating at the Federal Bureau of Investiga-

MCIC NUMBER_____

Florida Department of Law Enforcement MCIC Report Form #1

NAME (LAST, FIRST, MIDDLE) | ALIAS/NICKNAMES

| SEX ☐ M ☐ F | RACE ☐ WHITE ☐ AMERICAN INDIAN OR ALASKAN NATIVE ☐ BLACK ☐ ASIAN OR PACIFIC ISLANDER | ☐ HISPANIC ☐ NON-HISPANIC | DATE OF BIRTH MO/DAY/YR | AGE |

| HEIGHT | WEIGHT | EYE COLOR ☐ BLACK ☐ BROWN | ☐ BLUE ☐ GRAY | ☐ GREEN ☐ HAZEL | ☐ MAROON ☐ PINK |

| HAIR COLOR | ☐ BLACK ☐ BROWN | ☐ BLOND ☐ RED | HAIR LENGTH | ☐ EAR ☐ COLLAR | ☐ SHOULDER ☐ BELOW SHOULDER |

| HAIR STYLE | ☐ AFRO ☐ CURLY | ☐ STRAIGHT ☐ BRAIDED/PONYTAIL | FACIAL HAIR | ☐ NONE ☐ UNSHAVEN | ☐ BEARD ☐ MUSTACHE ☐ GOATEE ☐ SIDEBURNS |

| COMPLEXION | ☐ ALBINO ☐ BLACK | ☐ FAIR, LIGHT ☐ MEDIUM | ☐ DARK ☐ RUDDY | BUILD | ☐ THIN ☐ MEDIUM | ☐ HEAVY ☐ MUSCULAR |

| TEETH | ☐ NORMAL | ☐ GAPS | ☐ GOLDCAPPED | ☐ CHIPPED | ☐ PROTRUDING | ☐ DECAYED |

SCARS, MARKS, DEFORMITIES (Describe and indicate location on body, including tattoos)

| SOCIAL SECURITY NUMBER | DRIVER'S LICENSE NUMBER | FINGERPRINT CLASSIFICATION |

| DATE AND TIME LAST SEEN MO/DAY/YR ☐ AM ☐ PM | LOCATION LAST SEEN (CITY, STATE) | POSSIBLE DIRECTION OF TRAVEL (CITY, STATE) |

LAST SEEN WEARING (HAT, SHIRT, GLASSES, PANTS, JEWELRY, ETC.)

| IN COMPANY WITH (NAME AND AGE) | PRESENT MENTAL STATE ☐ DEPRESSED ☐ AMNESIA ☐ SUICIDAL ☐ OTHER_____ |

| MEDICATION REQUIRED ☐ YES ☐ NO | REASON _____ TYPE |

| DENTAL RECORDS AVAILABLE ☐ YES ☐ NO | DOCTORS' RECORDS (X-RAYS, ETC.) ☐ YES ☐ NO AVAILABLE | MISSING ORGANS | BLOOD TYPE |

| VEHICLE TYPE | MAKE | MODEL | YEAR | TAG NUMBER | TAG STATE | COLORS (EXTERIOR/INTERIOR) |

OTHER IDENTIFYING CHARACTERISTICS OF VEHICLE

BACKGROUND INFORMATION

HOBBIES AND INTERESTS (DANCING, SWIMMING, SURFING, FISHING, ETC.)

ASSOCIATIONS (CLUBS, ORGANIZATIONS, GANGS, ETC.)

TYPE HANGOUTS FREQUENTED (COUNTRY BARS, VIDEO ARCADES, DISCOS, BOWLING ALLEYS, SKATING RINKS, ETC.)

EXHIBIT TWO

PLEASE INCLUDE ANY PERTINENT INFORMATION REGARDING THE MISSING CHILD NOT ADDRESSED ELSEWHERE ON THIS FORM.

_____

_____

_____

_____

_____

_____

SEND COMPLETED FORM TO: Florida Department of Law Enforcement, Missing Children Information Clearinghouse, Post Office Box 1489, Tallahassee, Florida 32302

IF POSSIBLE, ENCLOSE A WALLET SIZE, CURRENT PHOTOGRAPH OF MISSING CHILD.

MCIC USE ONLY

PARENT/GUARDIAN NAME		DATE RECEIVED	DATE ENTERED MCIC	DATE REMOVED MCIC
PARENT/GUARDIAN ADDRESS		ENTERED FCIC ☐ YES ☐ NO	CANCELLED FCIC ☐ YES ☐ NO	DATE PUBLISHED
PARENT/GUARDIAN PHONE NUMBER		DATE OF EMANCIPATION		
LOCAL AGENCY HANDLING CASE	CASE NUMBER	DISPOSITION		
ADDRESS				
PHONE NUMBER				

PLEASE NOTIFY MCIC AS SOON AS POSSIBLE AFTER LOCATION OF CHILD HAS BEEN DETERMINED.
1-800-342-0821

undersigned _____
(print name and relationship, parent, spouse, legal guardian, etc)
_____ , hereby requests that his/her
ne, age, description, photograph (enclosed), and circumstances surrounding his/her
issing status appear in the law enforcement bulletin published by the Florida Depart-
nt of Law Enforcement I understand this information will be published in more than
·10 reports, made available to law enforcement, hospitals, medical examiners.
· dren shelters, social services, and other agencies or organizations involved with
sing children.

further understood and agreed that any and all information supplied by me shall be
hful, and I agree to hold harmless the Florida Department of Law Enforcement, for
errors of omission or commission occasioned by misinformation I may supply

The undersigned individual(s) placing the description of a child in the law enforcement
bulletin agrees to indemnify and hold harmless the Florida Department of Law Enforcement, and any and all Law Enforcement Agencies or other organizations and/or individuals, contacts or sources of information, for or on account of any Legal Liability for
suits, actions, claims or damages that the reported missing child might prosecute
against the aforesaid persons and entities and/or individuals, whether successful or un-
successful, including defendants costs sustained.

SIGNED: _____

DATED: _____

tion academy at Quantico, Virginia. Local police departments can send standardized reports on murders, such as those involving missing children, to VICAP. The data are then entered into a computer and specialists look for common threads among the cases. VICAP aims at tracking down the offenders, including those who are killing very large numbers of children, constituting yet another approach to the problem of missing children.

STATE LAW ENFORCEMENT AGENCIES GET TO WORK

New and outstanding work in the police departments of some major cities and states is setting a good example for other law enforcement agencies. For example, the 1982 Florida Legislature appropriated funds for the establishment of a Missing Children Information Clearinghouse (MCIC). Many of the clearinghouse services acted as a model for other programs. (See Exhibit 2.)

The Kentucky Task Force on Exploited and Missing Children was a pioneer in responding to the growing national tragedy of missing children. The final report of this task force, which was published in 1983, explores the problem at the national level, as well as in Kentucky. It includes eighteen recommendations for actions that are needed to better safeguard "Kentucky's vulnerable children."

The Indianapolis Police Department's missing person's unit was created in 1968; but when Sergeant Joe St. John took over the unit in 1978 he found that there was much improvement needed. By 1983, Indianapolis's record for solving cases of missing children was outstanding. Much of this success can be attributed to the use of the media in Indianapolis, where television stations air photos of missing children, radio stations give descriptions, and newspapers publish pictures. The Police Department issues a monthly bulletin of missing children, sends copies to police departments in nearby communities, and posts copies in areas that are popular with runaways. The Indianapolis police have an excellent record in immediate response when a child is reported missing. They also make good use of the FBI's National Crime Information Center computer, the system made available by the Missing Children's Act. Captain Lawrence Turner, formerly head of the Juvenile Branch, says that Indianapolis is proud of its record in finding its missing children, but any city where people are concerned and work together can do the same thing.

TEENAGERS CAN HELP

Just a few of the many programs and legislation in which people are coping with the problem of missing children have been mentioned in this book. Even though some strides are being made, the problem is so great that it will not be easily solved.

There is much that *you* can do as an individual and/or with a group to which you belong. For example, you can enlist the help of the National Center for Missing and Exploited Children in providing instruction packets that aid communities in protecting children, and distribute them through your local parent-teacher organizations. You can encourage organizations to use the outreach program of public speaking and the prevention and education programs for schools that the National Center provides. You can encourage schools to introduce a call-back system so that the school day does not elapse before a search begins. You can encourage local media to carry pictures of missing children and dairies to put their pictures on milk cartons.

You can help to introduce information on crime prevention and the whole problem of missing children and teens in your community by organizing a Child Safety Day. You can help to publicize Missing Children's Day. This is May 25th, the anniversary of the disappearance of Etan Patz. And you can help to publicize Family Reunion Month.

You can find out what is being done in your area to help

in the search for missing children. To what degree are law enforcement agencies using the help available from the National Center on Missing and Exploited Children? How is this agency helping educators in your area? These actions and many more that have already been suggested in this book can help to make a difference so that children and young people will be safer in the future.

SOURCES OF FURTHER INFORMATION

HOTLINES CONCERNED WITH MISSING CHILDREN AND RUNAWAYS

CHILD FIND NATIONAL HOTLINE
1-800-431-5005

NATIONAL CHILD SAFETY COUNCIL
1-800-222-1464

NATIONAL CENTER FOR MISSING CHILDREN
1-800-843-5678

    COUNSELING STAFF
    1-202-634-9821

NATIONAL RUNAWAY HOTLINE
1-800-621-4000

RUNAWAY HOTLINE
1-800-231-6946

ACTION AGENCIES

Many of these agencies may be temporary. Do not be discouraged if some do not respond. Continue to try local and national groups.

ABDUCTED CHILDREN
INFORMATION CENTER (ACIC)
1470 Gene Street, Winter Park, FL 32789. 305-831-2000.
Computerized registry for missing and abducted children operated at no charge by Locater's International, Inc.

ADAM WALSH CHILD RESOURCE CENTER, INC.
1876 North University Drive, Fort Lauderdale, FL 33322. 305-475-4847.
Working for missing, abused, and neglected children.

BAY AREA CENTER FOR VICTIMS
OF CHILD STEALING
1165 Meridian Avenue, Suite 112, San Jose, CA 95125. *CHAPTERS:* South Bay, 408-972-2910. North Bay, 707-544-6536. East Bay, 415-276-2679. Monterey Bay, 408-425-5134.
A nonprofit organization composed of parents and concerned citizens. The primary goals are to educate the public to the crime of child stealing and provide support and help for victims. Activities include consultation, referrals, media involvement, lectures, expert witnesses, poster distribution, monthly meetings, and telephone hotlines for victim parents. There is a $20.00 annual membership fee.

BERGEN COUNTY MISSING PERSONS BUREAU
1 Court Street, Hackensack, NJ 07601. 201-646-2192.
Maintains perhaps the largest data bank in the United States on unidentified bodies.

CENTER FOR THE FAMILY IN TRANSITION
5725 Paradise Drive, Building A, Suite 100, Corte Madera, CA 94925. 415-924-5750.
Serves children and families of the Bay Area involved in parental child stealing. Provides victim counseling.

CHILD FIND
P.O. Box 277, New Paltz, NY 12561. 914-255-1848.
Distributes *Child Find* magazine to schools/officials; communicates to children through schools/public media. Does computerized matching of children with registered parents. Has extremely good relationship with national media. Sponsors Missing Children's Day.

CHILD FIND, INC. (Utah Chapter)
1009 East 4555 Street, Salt Lake City, UT 84117. Salt Lake City, 801-262-8056. Salt Lake City, 801-268-1949. Salt Lake City, 801-467-6415. Provo, 801-375-5135.
Gives talks on prevention of child abductions.

CHILD INDUSTRIES
P.O. Box 26814, Salt Lake City, UT 84126. 801-298-2902.
A nonprofit corporation dedicated to the prevention of cruelty to children. One of the programs is the "PAT" (Prevention Awareness Techniques) Family Program. With this package parents and children are educated through a home study program designed to protect children from potentially dangerous situations and people.

CHILDREN'S RIGHTS OF FLORIDA, INC.
P.O. Box 173, Pinellas Park, FL 33565. 813-546-1593.
A nonprofit organization dedicated to helping parents in locating and/or recovering their abducted children (both parental and stranger abductions), also runaways. Goal is to bring all missing children home to safety once again. Works within the legal system to aid parents in dealing with the "red

tape" that is so very prevalent in this problem. Supports proposed legislation and are constantly updating awareness of new legislation that is passed to aid the searching parent. Claims to have been instrumental in the location and recovery of 60 children in past year.

CHILDREN'S RIGHTS OF PENNSYLVANIA, INC.
P.O. Box 2764, Lehigh Valley, PA 18001. 215-437-2971.
Goal is to aid parents and guardians in finding their missing children. Puts together and circulates an up-to-date picture exhibit of children who have been abducted either by a parent or an unknown person. Photographs and information should be sent to above address.

CHILD SEARCH
6 Beacon Street, Suite 600, Boston, MA 02108. 617-720-1750.
A new idea for an old problem—believes abducted children can be found quickly and inexpensively through the public school systems of the United States. Publishes a magazine-like paper for distribution to 100,000 public schools.

CHILD WATCH—USA
P.O. Box 17211, 3815 Interstate Court, Suite 201, Montgomery, AL 36117. 205-271-5200.
Setting up 26 separate regional offices to maintain a 24-hour nationwide toll-free service. Each regional director is responsible for contacting the nearest field representative or volunteer to the caller, making personal contact with the parent and obtaining all information required to begin an actual physical search for the child.

COALITION ORGANIZED FOR
PARENTAL EQUALITY (COPE)
68 Deering Street, Portland, ME 04101. 207-775-0258.
COPE maintains the card file for the *National Congress for Men Directory*, which lists all active divorce reform, parental

rights, men's issues, child location, and sources of divorce mediation in the United States, Canada, and some foreign countries.

COBRA CONNECTION
P.O. Box 7016, Station A, Canton, OH 44705-0958. 216-454-9109.
Publishes and distributes 46-page manual "Save a Child" that informs, instructs, creates awareness of the missing phenomenon, and teaches prevention; also distributes a flyer for children and interested groups. Also makes public appearances.

E.C.H.O. (Exploited Children's Help Organization)
1204 South 3rd Street, Suite B, Louisville, KY 40203. 502-637-8761.
Interested in increasing awareness about the problems of missing and exploited children. Working aggressively to provide enough information to prevent more tragedies from occurring, to provide parental support to those who have missing children and to pursue laws in support of and to protect our children.

FIND THE CHILDREN
11811 W. Olympic Boulevard, Los Angeles, CA 90064. 800-KID-FIND.
Nonprofit organization founded by the film producer Linda Otto. See page 70 for objectives.

FIND-ME, INC.
P.O. Box 1612, LaGrange, GA 30241-1612. 404-884-7419.
Information center for families with a missing member; counsels families; promotes awareness and information to media and public. Interested in all ages and types of disappearances; specializes in older teens and adults—a group that gets the least media and public attention and concern. Publishes ACTION booklet. Sponsors Family Reunion Month.

Has no payroll or other administrative expense, therefore 100% of receipts used in promoting awareness of and solutions to the missing persons phenomenon. Makes annual report to contributors.

FRIENDS OF CHILD FIND (of Maine)
P.O. Box 3772, Portland, ME 04104. 207-775-2430.

FRIENDS OF CHILD FIND (of Montana)
725 South Billings Boulevard, No. 0, Billings, MT 59101. 406-259-6999.

FRIENDS OF CHILD FIND (of Oregon)
P.O. Box 756, Springfield, OR 97477-0131.
Promotes awareness through public presentations and abduction prevention programs. Serves as an information and referral service.

GALLERY 345/ART FOR SOCIAL CHANGE, INC.
345 Lafayette Street, New York, NY 10012. 212-535-4797.
Has a project, "Children in Crisis," through which it promotes awareness through exhibits of missing children, teens, and young adults. You may submit information and photographs of your child free of charge. The exhibit can be used by any group as an awareness project. There is no charge other than shipping involved. Does not include parental child snatching.

H.E.A.R.T. (Help Every Abduction Return Today)
10937 Red Arrow Highway, Route 1, Mattawan, MI 49071. 616-668-3733.
Nonprofit Michigan-based self-help organization for families victimized by parental child snatching; major interests include legislative lobby, fingerprinting drives, recovery follow-up, support and referral outreach, and cooperation with search organizations nationwide.

HIDE AND SEEK FOUNDATION, INC.
P.O. Box 806, McMinnville, OR 97218. 503-662-3620 or 503-472-3717.
A nonprofit organization that undertakes an investigation of each individual case at *no* cost to the searching family. Offers crisis counseling; promotes awareness through public speaking to schools, organizations, churches, and clubs interested in what to do if someone disappears from the family unit; educates the community on abduction precautions, preventive measures, and legal issues concerning custody matters; supports legislation for children's rights and budget increases for law enforcement agencies to add the additional manpower needed to help locate missing children; supports legislation against child stealing; accepts donations, gifts, and grants.

HIDE AND SEEK OF ALAMEDA CO.
4456 Doane Street, Fremont, CA 94538. 415-656-6792.

HIDE AND SEEK OF CAMDEN CO.
150 Berlin Road, Gibbsboro, NJ 08026. 609-783-3101.

HIDE AND SEEK OF FAIRBANKS
SR Box 80292, Fairbanks, AK 99701. 907-488-3591.

HIDE AND SEEK OF PA
c/o Woodward Caves, Woodward, PA 16882. 814-349-5185.

HIDE AND SEEK HELP LINE
503-472-4333.
Crisis counseling, assists victimized families.

KYLE'S STORY
205 North Chilton Avenue, LaGrange, GA 30240. 404-884-7419.
Supplements FIND-ME in areas FIND-ME is prohibited by IRS regulations to work. Assists in publishing ACTION book-

let. Named for *Kyle's Story: Friday Never Came. The Search for Missing People,* which relates problems encountered in getting officials and the general public to accept the possibility that the disappearance of a college student could foretell a problem. NBC calls *Kyle's Story* "one of the best overall treatments of 'the missing phenomenon.' "

MISSING CHILDREN . . . HELP CENTER
410 Ware Boulevard, Suite 1102, Tampa, FL 33619. 813-681-HELP or 813-623-KIDS.
Reference and referral agency for families of missing children. Speaker's bureau to educate the public. Twenty-four-hour HELP line. Distribution of vital missing children posters nationwide. All services free of charge.

MISSING CHILDREN OF AMERICA, INC.
P.O. Box 10-1938, Anchorage, AK 99510. 907-243-8484.
"A National Network to Locate Missing Children." Educates through seminars, workshops, etc.; locates through referrals to detectives; identifies with "Know Your Child" package.

MISSING PERSONS NATIONWIDE, INC.
P.O. Box 5331, Hudson, FL 33568. 813-856-5144.
Provides assistance in locating missing persons of all ages.

MISSING TEENS AND YOUNG ADULTS
P.O. Box 7800, Santa Cruz, CA 95061. 408-425-3663 or 408-426-7972.
Forming a nationwide group of parents of missing teens and young adults for purpose of helping each other.

NATIONAL ASSOCIATION FOR
MISSING CHILDREN, INC.
300 South University Drive, Plantation, FL 33324. 305-473-6126.
Association of parents and others concerned about child abduction. To publish a three-part Child Safe Program con-

sisting of Parent Guide Book, Child Pac, data card system, and Parents Action Plan.

NATIONAL CENTER FOR
MISSING AND EXPLOITED CHILDREN
1835 K Street, N.W., Washington, DC 20006. 202-634-9821.
Distributes action plans for parents, effective searching techniques, American Bar Association Noncustodial Parent Abduction Packet, National Directory of Nonprofit Action Citizen Organizations, to searching parents and law enforcement agencies.

NATIONAL COALITION FOR
CHILDREN'S JUSTICE
2998 Shelburne Road, Shelburne, VT 05482. 802-985-8458.
Promotes awareness through journalism/public speaking. Investigative ABC News correspondent for "20/20." Developing a computerized NATIONAL CHILD VICTIM NETWORK.

NATIONAL "KID PRINT" PROGRAM
P.O. Box 5548, Buena Park, CA 90622. 714-983-0945.
A program of Orange County Search and Rescue. Provides information on establishing a local print program that is compatible and identifiable with FBI computers. Services also include putting parents in contact with other organizations.

NATIONAL MISSING CHILDREN'S
LOCATE CENTER, INC.
P.O. Box 42584, Portland, OR 97242. 503-238-1350.
Publishes *The Can: Children's Action Network Directory*. Sponsors Family Reunion Month.

NATIONAL ORGANIZATION
FOR VICTIM ASSISTANCE
1757 Park Road, N.W., Washington, DC 20010.
Provides help to the parents of children stolen by another spouse in getting through the legal maze of bringing a child back, after they have located the child.

NATIONWIDE MISSING PERSONS BUREAU
3500 Aldine Bender, Box A, Houston, TX 77032. 713-449-0355 or 713-449-3449.
Nationwide missing person's clearinghouse. In process of building a large building just south of Inter-Continental Airport to service any needs of missing persons, no matter what age group. This will include unidentified bodies, etc.

OKLAHOMA'S ABDUCTED CHILDREN, INC.
P.O. Box 21326, Oklahoma City, OK 73120. 405-842-7293.
Provides an immediate response to parents of abducted children, gives technical assistance and emotional support during and following recovery, promotes public awareness and supports needed legislation.

OKLAHOMA PARENTS
AGAINST CHILD STEALING
P.O. Box 2112, Bartlesville, OK 74005. 918-534-1489.
Provides personal assistance to the custodial parent in locating and recovery of their missing children, keeps informed of federal and state laws pertaining to missing children and makes these laws known to the victimized parent; actively supports other organizations concerned with missing children.

OPERATION GO-HOME
P.O. Box 12, Westport, Ontario K0G 1X0. 613-273-2046.
Canadian network for referrals from the missing child and/or parent.

PARENTS AGAINST
CHILD SNATCHING, INC.
P.O. Box 581, Coraopolis, PA 15108. 412-264-9025 or 412-526-5537.
Offers advice, counseling, and guidance to the parents of abducted children.

PARENTS AGAINST CHILD SNATCHING

5554 Cobb Meadow, Norcross, GA 30093. 404-921-8526.
Provides victim parents with emotional support and guidance in legal remedies. Supports pending legislation favorable to such cause. Works with local enforcement agencies to improve cooperative effort. Holds monthly meetings; accepts donations.

PARENTS OF MURDERED CHILDREN

1739 Bella Vista, Cincinnati, OH 45237. 513-721-LOVE or 513-242-8025.
Compassionate outreach program; a self-help support organization with groups for parents and other homicide survivors; chapters located throughout the United States.

PARENTS WITHOUT PARTNERS, INC.

7910 Woodmont Avenue, Suite 1000, Bethesda, MD 20814. 301-654-8850.
International organization dedicated to the welfare and interests of single parents and their children. For more information and location of nearest chapter call toll free 800-638-8078.

THE ROBERTA JO SOCIETY

129 East Main Street, Chillicothe, OH 45601. 614-772-1781.
Gathering statistics on missing children and unidentified bodies; offers counseling for victimized families; sought national clearinghouse for missing children under 18. Also makes Americans aware of child abductions through public speaking in churches, schools, and civic clubs; seeks attitude changes that aid victimized families; assists and guides families of missing children, emotionally and practically; publishes and mails flyers to sheriffs, schools, and police; informs news media. All guidance and information is given free of charge, whether through the mail or over the telephone. However, cannot accept any collect phone calls.

SEARCHING PARENTS
P.O. Box 19609, Portland, OR 97219. 503-246-0573.
Organization formed to assist parents of missing children to locate and recover those children.

SEARCHING PARENTS ASSOCIATION
P.O. Box 582, East Tawas, MI 48730. 517-362-7148.
Provides counseling to victimized parents of abducted children, children stolen by the noncustodial parent, parents of runaways, and parents who have recovered their children. Also available: at cost investigative help; at cost sighting verification; photo updating and distribution nationwide to other search groups; prevention information; speakers for civic groups; advice on recovering the missing children. Tax deductible donations are gratefully accepted.

SINGLE PARENT
7910 Woodmont Avenue, Suite 1008, Bethesda, MD 20814. 301-654-8850.
Publishes *Single Parent* magazine, which is interested in producing a list of contacts that help parents seeking recovery of their children with services, counseling, referrals, lobbying, and other special projects on the issue of child snatching.

SOCIETY FOR YOUNG VICTIMS
29 Thurston Avenue, Newport, RI 02840. 401-847-5083.
First organization to lobby for national information center; licensed detective; organizes search teams for police; maintains scrapbooks and computerized statistics. Affiliate of FIND-ME. Sponsors Family Reunion Month.

STOLEN CHILD INFORMATION EXCHANGE
2523 Daphne Place, Fullerton, CA 92633.
Claims to be only counseling organization that deals exclusively with parental kidnapping, enabling better understanding and explaining the problem; provides technical advice to many nationally televised programs.

EDWIN SHAW IV, INC.
615 East First Avenue, Chadbourn, NC 28431. 919-847-5083.
Can get information distributed through contacts in trucking industry. Sponsors Family Reunion Month.

ORGANIZATIONS EAGER TO ASSIST CHILD SAFETY FAIRS IN ANY APPROPRIATE WAY

ACTION—MISSING AND
EXPLOITED CHILDREN PROJECT
806 Connecticut Avenue, N.W., Room M-1007, Washington, DC 20525

AD COUNCIL
1730 Rhode Island Avenue, N.W., Washington, DC 20036;
825 Third Avenue, New York, NY 10022

ADAM WALSH CHILD RESOURCE CENTER
1876 N. University Drive, #306, Fort Lauderdale, FL 33322

AMERICAN ASSOCIATION OF
COMMUNITY & JUNIOR COLLEGES
One Dupont Circle, N.W., #410, Washington, DC 20036

AMERICAN ASSOCIATION OF RETIRED PERSONS
1909 K Street, N.W., Washington, DC 20049

AMERICAN BAR ASSOCIATION,
NATIONAL LEGAL RESOURCE CENTER
1800 M Street, N.W., Washington, DC 20036

THE AMERICAN LEGION,
AMERICANISM & CHILDREN & YOUTH
P.O. Box 1055, Indianapolis, IN 46206

BOYS CLUBS OF AMERICA
6501 Loisdale Court, Suite 901, Springfield, VA 22150

BOY SCOUTS OF AMERICA, EXPLORER DIVISION
1325 Walnut Hill Lane, Irving, TX 75062-1296

CHILD KEYPPERS OF FLORIDA
P.O. Box 6292, Lake Worth, FL 33466

GENERAL FEDERATION OF WOMEN'S CLUBS
1734 N Street, N.W., Washington, DC 20036

GIRL SCOUTS, USA
1625 I Street, N.W., #612, Washington, DC 20006

INTERNATIONAL ASSOCIATION OF CHIEFS OF POLICE
13 Firstfield Road, P.O. Box 6010, Gaithersburg, MD 20878

INTERNATIONAL ASSOCIATION OF FIRE CHIEFS
1329 18th Street, N.W., Washington, DC 20036

KIWANIS INTERNATIONAL
3636 Woodview Terrace, Indianapolis, IN 46268

NATIONAL CRIME PREVENTION COUNCIL
805 15th Street, N.W., #718, Washington, DC 20005

NATIONAL FRATERNAL ORDER OF POLICE
8035 Northwest 185 Terrace, Hialeah, FL 33015

NATIONAL SHERIFFS' ASSOCIATION
1250 Connecticut Avenue, N.W., #320, Washington, DC 20036

U.S. DEPARTMENT OF JUSTICE
Office of Juvenile Justice and Delinquency Prevention, 633 Indiana Avenue, N.W., Washington, DC 20531

SUGGESTED READING

Abrahams, Sally. *Children in the Crossfire: The Tragedy of Parental Kidnapping.* New York: Atheneum, 1983.

Agopian, Michael W. *Parental Child-Stealing.* Lexington, Massachusetts: Lexington Books, 1981.

Clinkscales, John D. *Kyle's Story: Friday Never Came. The Search for Missing People.* New York: Vantage Press, 1981.

Gill, John Edward. *Stolen Children.* New York: Seaview Books, 1981.

Gutcheon, Beth. *Still Missing.* New York: Dell, 1982 (fiction).

Harris, Marilyn. *The Runaway's Diary.* New York: Pocket Books, 1983 (fiction).

Hyde, Margaret O. *Cry Softly: The Story of Child Abuse.* Philadelphia, Pennsylvania: The Westminster Press, 1980.

_____. *My Friend Wants to Run Away.* New York: McGraw Hill, 1979.

_____. *Sexual Abuse: Let's Talk About It.* Philadelphia, Pennsylvania: Westminster Press, 1984.

Kosof, Anna. *Runaways.* New York: Franklin Watts, 1977.

Mazer, Norma Fox. *Taking Terri Mueller.* New York: Avon, 1981 (fiction).

Olsen, Jack. *Have You Seen My Son?* New York: Atheneum, 1982 (fiction).

Strickland, Margaret. *Childsnatched.* Moore Haven, New Jersey: Rainbow Books, 1979.

Wooden, Kenneth. *Prey: Missing and Murdered Children.* New York: McGraw-Hill. Soon to be published.

INDEX